MEETINGS WITH REMARKABLE TREES

Text and photographs by

THOMAS PAKENHAM

PHOENIX ILLUSTRATED

CONTENTS

Introduction • 6

Fig. III.

HALF TITLE PAGE Yews at Stow-on-the-Wold TITLE PAGE Beech at Tullynally

FRONT ENDPAPER Scots pines at Rothiemurchus BACK ENDPAPER Beech at Tullynally

SHRINES

FANTASIES

SURVIVORS

INTRODUCTION
MY BEST SIXTY

THIS IS NOT A CONVENTIONAL BOOK ABOUT TREES. IT

WILL NOT HELP YOU IDENTIFY THEM, LET ALONE

CULTIVATE THEM. IT'S A PERSONAL SELECTION OF 60

REMARKABLE INDIVIDUALS (OR GROUPS OF TREES)

MOSTLY VERY LARGE, AND MAINLY VERY ANCIENT, AND

ALL WITH A STRONG PERSONALITY.

It is these living (or dying) monuments that I have tried to portray with pen and camera. No one has produced a book of British tree portraits, I think, since Jacob Strutt's *Sylva Britannica* of 1826. And of course Strutt, a little-known artist, did not have the benefit of the camera.

I can trace the origins of this book to two experiences – encounters, if you like – of my own. The first was at home in Ireland, the second on the borders of Tibet.

Now I don't usually hug trees, but on the evening of 5 January 1991 I made an exception. For three days the weatherman on Irish television had been tracking an interesting hole in the Atlantic pressure system; he forecast, rather too cheerfully I thought, that a severe storm would hit Ireland early in the morning of 6 January. I

went out in the evening of the 5th and stood contemplating the old beeches in the garden: 19 of them. I guessed they were a little under 200 years old and 100 feet high. Why had I not looked at them more carefully before? The evening was absolutely still with the patch of red in the western sky that is supposed to delight shepherds. Pessimistically I put my faith in the weatherman. I slipped a tape measure round the smooth, silver-green, lichen-encrusted bellies of the trees and listed the measurements in a notebook. None was a record breaker. But all had been good friends to five generations of our family. As I taped each tree, I gave it a hug, as if to say 'good luck tonight'.

I awoke next morning to a noise like the sea, but a gale, not a hurricane. Rather an anticlimax, I thought – stupidly. When I went down to the garden, crunching over broken twigs and branches, the tallest beech lay there like a fallen sentry. All that day and the following night the gale persisted, with news of casualties coming in by telephone (oddly, the telephone line survived). Two of our oldest beech trees were straddling the main road; they were being cut up by the fire brigade. Another had sealed off the back drive. One had just missed the stable archway. I went out into the open parkland and watched, from as close as I dared, the trees facing their tormentors. The gusts struck each tree, or clump of trees, like a wave hitting the bow of a ship.

It reminded me of a night I once spent in a Force Ten storm in the North Sea, perched on the bridge of a trawler from Lowestoft. There would be a moment's struggle when you thought the bow would

Frontispiece for *Sylva Britannica* by Jacob Strutt (1826)

never lift; then the ship arched its back; with a juddering bang the spray flashed over the ship from bow-rail to stern. In the park, each time a gust hit a beech I thought it would capsize. Then it arched its back and was free. But 12, tall, ancient beech trees were ripped out of the ground before we heard the last of that storm.

The second encounter took place in November 1993 when I was plant-hunting in Yunnan, in south-west China, close to the border with Tibet. Yunnan is botanically one of the treasure chests of the world, as well as being stunningly beautiful. There are ten times more tree species in western Yunnan than in the whole of Britain and Ireland. We spent three weeks hunting maples, sorbus and birch – and dodging the logging trucks – in the mountainous border region where the peaks go up to 23,000 feet. One day our lorry brought us to a plateau full of giant rhododendrons and drooping juniper. Half an hour's walk down a path we were shown a giant Chinese hemlock spruce, *Tsuga dumosa.* It was so large, 33 feet in girth at breast height, that an old man had built a cabin among the roots. But the most remarkable thing about it struck me only after I had returned home. It was the first – and last – very large tree we saw in the wild in the whole of Yunnan. All the other large, ancient trees (away from the precincts of Buddhist temples) had been taken by the loggers. Yet this giant hemlock, unique in south-west Yunnan, was probably smaller, at least in volume of timber, than a large beech tree that it is commonplace to find in a fine park in Britain or Ireland.

From both encounters I drew the same lesson. We tend to take our large, old trees for granted. When they fall we feel a pang of bereavement. But it should not need an Atlantic storm in Ireland, or the hurricanes that hit southern England in 1987 and 1990, or even the new bypass that is ripping the heart out of Newbury, to teach us to appreciate old trees.

The only large ancient tree left alive by the loggers: a 33-feet-girth hemlock in Yunnan, China

In Britain and Ireland, as Oliver Rackham has shown, we have inherited a richer legacy of old trees than any other people in western Europe. The French cut theirs down with cool efficiency. (Among the exceptions are the 300-year-old veterans in the forest of Tronçais, near Moulins, honoured with the names of outstanding Frenchmen. 'Marshal Pétain', named in 1918, was recently rechristened 'Hero of the Resistance'.) By contrast we have had a soft spot for old trees since the time of Shakespeare – or so we like to think.

I travelled the length and breadth of Britain and Ireland doing research for this book. Away from gardens and arboreta, many of the ancient trees that I saw were suffering from neglect. Fences, put up years ago to protect them from sheep, cattle and horses, were often broken and useless. I do not blame landowners. Often the task is beyond them. They receive little help from the authorities. There are few signposts to any of the trees in this book; in fact few ancient trees have ever been put on the Ordnance Survey. And few historians have troubled themselves much about these monuments – with the honourable exceptions of Oliver Rackham and Sir Keith Thomas.

Yet old trees are living documents; when they die they can be dated from the annual rings, unless the core is hollow; even then it may be easier to date them than a building. Most depressing was the experience of finding 1,000-year-old trees, once famous and well cared for, now left to their fate, like the yews at Lorton and Borrowdale in Cumbria, whose bark is being stripped by local sheep.

The indifference towards old trees makes a mockery of our supposed new respect for the environment. Consider the raw facts. The giants of our native species – oak, ash and beech – are the biggest living things on these islands: heavier than any land animal, taller than most buildings, older than many ancient monuments. If a big tree was not a living organism it would still be a remarkable object. A big oak or beech can weigh 30 tons, cover 2,000 square yards, include ten miles of twigs and branches. Each year the tree pumps several tons of water about 100 feet into the air, produces a new crop of

100,000 leaves and covers half an acre of trunk and branches with a new pelt of bark. Yet the tree is alive. There is no mass production: every tree, sexually conceived, is built to a different design – as we see at first glance.

And nowhere are these astonishing objects to be found in more profusion than close to where millions live. They are the wonders we take for granted, shading the village green, crowding the park, dominating the landscape.

In the past we have been complacent – with tragic results. Look at the views of southern England as we know them from the painters of the last two centuries: Salisbury painted by Constable, Petworth by Turner. The English elm dominates each of these landscapes, 'immemorial' in Tennyson's phrase. And now we can hardly remember them.

Those trees have gone the way of the dodo (apart from some dogged survivors around Brighton), killed by a fungus brought by an immigrant bark beetle carelessly imported from North America.

How did I choose the 60 trees, and groups of trees, for this book? Anyone interested in trees would have made a different selection. But this is my choice from thousands. I found these 60 remarkable in age, size, form, historical interest, or the use to which they were put. I have chosen them as an anthologist would cull his literary flowers, or an architectural writer would choose his 1,000 'best' buildings. I set myself only two rules. All trees had to be alive (or dead on their feet) in Britain or Ireland. They had also to be photogenic – or at least accessible to my camera. Roughly two thirds of the collection consists of ancient native trees, one third of exotic newcomers from Europe, the East and North America. The natives include only six out of the 35 species normally considered by botanists to be indigenous – meaning that they came to Britain unassisted after the last Ice Age. But these are the six that grow biggest and live longest: common oak, ash, beech, yew, Scots pine

and birch. A seventh giant, the sessile oak (*Quercus petraea*), common in western Britain and southern Ireland, has failed to be included. As a token of my respect, I include a photograph of the champion sessile oak, a tree at Croft Castle, Herefordshire, 37 feet in girth above the lowest branch.

My selection ranges from the cavernous Bowthorpe Oak in Lincolnshire, to three ancient Scots pines at Rothiemurchus, remnants of the Caledonian Forest. Among the exotics, in the section called *Travellers*, the trees from North America are dominant. These are the new champions of British and Irish woods, replacing those that were brought from Europe hundreds of years ago. The tallest Douglas fir, the 212-feet-high specimen at the Hermitage, Dunkeld, is the tallest tree yet recorded in these islands. And who knows, it may one day top 300 feet – the height it has reached at its home in Oregon. The tree is hardly more than 100 years old and rising like a space rocket. In the final section, *Survivors*, I contrast ancients like the 'Conqueror's Oak' at Windsor with an amazing Chinese newcomer, the *Metasequoia glyptostroboides*. This newcomer was discovered as a fossil by a Japanese palaeobotanist in 1941, and only a few months later was found to be alive and well and living in a remote corner of south-west China. Today the 70-feet-high specimens at Cambridge Botanic Garden are only 48 years old but have already the gnarled roots of veterans. The Conqueror's Oak has been dying for about 300 years but has still a large head of fresh green leaves.

To visit these trees, to step beneath their domes and vaults, is to pay homage at a mysterious shrine. But tread lightly. Even these giants have delicate roots. And be warned that this may be your farewell visit. No one can say if this prodigious trunk will survive the next Atlantic storm – or outlive us all by centuries.

To hunt out and photograph these trees, that punctuate the landscape from Kerry to Tayside, I depended on the knowledge, goodwill and enthusiasm of numerous experts. No one gave more

The champion sessile oak at Croft Castle, Herefordshire – 37 feet in girth

generous supplies of all three than Alan Mitchell, for many years
Britain's leading tree guru, though sadly he died before this book was
finished. For botanical advice, and unflinching criticism of every
sort, I have relied on Charles Nelson, formerly taxonomist at the
National Botanic Gardens, Glasnevin, Dublin. Other botanists to
whom I am especially grateful include Matthew Jebb, Keith
Rushforth, Keith Lamb, Donal Synnott, Stephen Spongberg,
Thomas Ward and David Hunt. I should also like to thank the staff
of the Royal Archives, (Windsor), the Kew Herbarium library, and
Brent Elliott and the staff of the RHS library. I am much indebted
to Kenneth Rose who added polish to the text.

I must acknowledge the help of the following landowners who
generously allowed me to photograph trees for this book: Alec
Blanchard, the owners of Fredville estate, David Hutton-Bury, the
City of London, John and Philippa Grant, John Noble, Lord and
Lady Cavendish, Forest Enterprise, the Earl of Mansfield, the
National Trust, George Clive, the Fellows of Emmanuel College
(Cambridge), the Headmaster of Bryanston School, Julian Williams,
the Heligan Trust, the owners of Rossdohan, the Office of Public
Works (Ireland), Lord and Lady De L'Isle, the owners of Pitchford
Hall, the Welbeck estate, Bicton College, the Marquess of
Lansdowne, Robert Steuart-Fothringham, Tom Hudson, the Earl of
Balfour, Knap Hill Gardens, the Crown Estate Commissioners, the
Earl of Erne, the Duke and Duchess of Devonshire, the Royal
Botanic Gardens (Kew), Dorset County Council, the Earl of March
and Goodwood estate, the Vicar of St Edward's, Stow-on-the-Wold
and the Vicar of St Peter's, Harlington. I would also like to thank
the following landowners who showed me remarkable trees: the
Duke of Wellington, Lord and Lady Tollemache, Bill Kemball, the
late Duke of Atholl and the Earl of Cromarty.

Friends who gave me generous hospitality while I was working on
the book include: Joy Blois-Brooke, Jim and Barbara Bailey, Patrick
and Anthea Forde, Jane Martineau and Willy Mostyn-Owen, Alice
and Simon Boyd, Christopher and Jenny Bland, Lindy Dufferin,
Moira Woods, Richard and Olivia Keane, Caroline and Gathorne
Cranbrook, Michael and Dina Murphy, Richard and Liz Scarbrough,
James and Alison Spooner, Jacky and Julian Thompson, Patrick and
Kate Kavanagh, Linda and Laurence Kelly, Tricia and Timothy
Daunt. I am particularly grateful to Edith Spink and Diana Rowan
Rockefeller who smoothed my path among the arboreta of North
America. The following friends were full of advice and comfort: Billa
Harrod, Mark and Dorothy Girouard, Nella and Stan Opperman,
Pilly Cowell, Maurice and Rosemary Foster, Liam and Maureen
O'Flanagan. My family were, as usual, generous to a fault. My
parents read and criticized much of the text and helped select the
photographs. Of my 39 brothers, sisters, children, nephews, nieces,
great-nephews and great-nieces, I should like to single out those who
gave especial help: my sisters, Antonia, Judith and Rachel; my
brothers, Paddy, Michael and Kevin; all four of my children, Maria,
Eliza, Ned and Fred (who took the cover photograph); and my
godson, Benjie, and his wife Lucy, herself a brilliant photographer.

I must thank Anthony Cheetham and all the staff of Weidenfeld and
Orion for taking so much trouble to make this book a reality,
especially Emma Way, Richard Atkinson, Nick Clark, Caroline Earle
and Michael Dover. Once again I record my gratitude to Mike Shaw,
my agent, and all at Curtis Brown. Tragically, Joe Fox, the editor and
friend at Random House on whom I had depended for 30 years,
died before he could see the typescript. I am greatly in the debt of
numerous people, sometimes complete strangers, who found
themselves pressed into service as photographic models to give scale
to the trees. I must thank my friend Angelo Hornak who first
suggested that I took the photographs myself. He told me the camera
that would be best for the job was the Linhof Technika, but 'you
wouldn't be able to use it'. Of course I found the challenge
irresistible. And how can I ever repay my wife, Valerie, not addicted
to trees herself; her zeal in editing this book was all the more valiant.

Survivors from the elm plague:

English elms at Brighton

PART ONE

NATIVES

BRITISH &
IRISH GIANTS

THOU WERT A BAUBLE ONCE, A CUP AND BALL

WHICH BABES MIGHT PLAY WITH;

AND THE THIEVISH JAY,

SEEKING HER FOOD, WITH EASE MIGHT HAVE PURLOINED

THE AUBURN NUT...

William Cowper, *The Yardley oak*, 1791

PREVIOUS PAGE Fredville 'Majesty', co-champion oak of Britain

The Fredville Oak, from Sylva Britannica *by J. G. Strutt, 1825.*

INCOGNITO AT FREDVILLE

THE TWO LARGEST COMMON OAKS (*QUERCUS ROBUR*) IN

BRITAIN AND IRELAND – AND PROBABLY EUROPE, TOO –

ARE THE FREDVILLE OAK IN KENT AND THE

BOWTHORPE OAK IN LINCOLNSHIRE.

Both have grown awesomely large in rich farmland with a relatively warm summer: they are co-champions in girth, both measuring 40 feet, give or take a few inches. Otherwise they are opposites. The Fredville Oak is tall and still strikingly beautiful. The Bowthorpe Oak is more like a cave than a tree; a cavern with branches growing from its roof (see page 174).

Fredville was the place I visited first. It was a sunny January morning in 1994, and the scrubby woods were alive with pheasants, reared in the sheds behind the tree. The keeper took me round, proud of the giant.

I brought a copy of the sketches Jacob Strutt made of 'Majesty' in 1820. Majesty was the romantic name used for the tree in the early 19th century, and perhaps long before. It's a good title, though the tree adds to the grace of a monarch the scale of a mammoth. And Majesty proved to be astonishingly like its portrait taken by Strutt 174 years earlier. You have only to compare the photograph with Strutt's engraving to see how the tree seems to have lost hardly a branch in the interim. So it appears looking at its south face.

Go to the north face of the tree and you are confronted with a lofty void. The main trunk is hollow for its entire height, perhaps 30 feet. If you looked up from inside, you would see the blue of the sky, as though you were looking up the inside of a ruined tower.

Who planted Majesty, and when? I asked the locals in the village pub, a mile away. No one had even heard of the tree. For, strange as it may seem, Majesty is now living incognito at Fredville. As for Majesty's age, my guess is that it is medieval, or Elizabethan at the latest; to have reached maturity two centuries ago she could hardly be less. But no one will ever know, as Majesty has long outlived the houses and the squires whose lawns it once graced.

The Fredville Oak

A TREE LIKE
A DRAWING BY
THURBER

ASH TREES HAVE TO MAKE THEIR OWN WAY IN THE

WORLD, RESENTED BY GARDENERS AND FORESTERS

BECAUSE OF THEIR GREEDY OFFSPRING.

Every year millions of ash 'keys' – long, thin, winged seeds – literally fall by the wayside. But when they find sanctuary among the thorns of a hedgerow, what elegance they bring to a dull landscape (provided an ivy plant is not sharing the same sanctuary, as it often is). In winter a large ash rises like a pillar of fluted grey marble, and its black-budded branches descend like swags of grey plaster.

The ash at Clapton Court, Somerset does not, however, have any pretensions to elegance. Its reputation is based on its distended belly: measured at five feet from the ground its girth is 29 feet. This makes it the champion ash in girth now known in Britain or Ireland. Does it deserve the gold medal? Above the conventional measuring height, the trunk tapers like an egg or a carbuncle. Perhaps it should be placed in a separate class for the grotesque. There are plenty of pot-bellied oaks in the same class.

However, I must admit that a surreal quality redeems the wayward proportions of the Clapton Ash. Its bark is the texture of stone. Is that a huge mossy boulder squatting on the lawn? Or (more alarmingly) some gigantic family pet as drawn by Thurber?

The Clapton Ash

HOPING FOR IMMORTALITY

AFTER TWO CENTURIES, WHEN MOST BEECHES ARE DEAD OR IN THEIR DOTAGE, A YEW IS A MERE STRIPLING. AT FIVE CENTURIES IT IS IN ITS PRIME. SOME MAY REACH THEIR MILLENIUM. SUCH IS THE EXTRAORDINARY LONGEVITY OF OUR NATIVE YEW (*TAXUS BACCATA*), THE OLDEST LIVING THING, AS FAR AS WE KNOW, IN EUROPE OR ASIA.

In the churchyard at Tandridge, Surrey, a mile from the M25 motorway, is a yew which appears to share with the parishioners the hope of immortality. Close to the ground the tree has a girth of over 34 feet, then divides into three huge trunks. The leaf canopy covers like a pall the whole western side of the churchyard, graves and all. Where its branches touch the ground they take root to form new trees.

How old is an old yew like this one at Tandridge? I asked Alan Mitchell, the dendrologist who spent 40 years scouring Britain and Ireland for champion trees. 'A good rule of thumb', he replied, 'is that most trees look older than they are except for yews which are even older than they look.'

But why not simply resolve the question of age by counting the annual rings of the trunk? In principle you can date most trees to the year they were born by this method, either by boring the trunks with an auger or by cutting the trees down. Neither auger nor axe is recommended to tree-lovers. But the auger has shown that the oldest living tree yet discovered is more than 4,000 years old: a stunted bristlecone pine called 'Old Methuselah' at the top of a mountain in California. Scientists bored its trunk and counted over 4,000 rings.

The axe made brutally clear that several of the giant Wellingtonias felled after their discovery in California in 1852 had lived over 3,000 years.

However, if the tree is particularly old, neither method works in western Europe. Our damp climate rots the heartwood of even the most durable native wood: yew. So there are no annual rings at the core of the Tandridge yew, just a void eight feet in diameter, big enough to stable a horse or park a car. All one could do in theory is to bore the outer shell and count the surviving rings; the ring count would probably only come to 300 or 400, but some yew wood is too hard for an auger to penetrate and then be removable.

At Tandridge, it is true, there is some tantalizing extra evidence. Archaeologists have found that a Saxon vault under the west wall, a relic of the first church, was deliberately skewed. Was this to avoid the roots of the yew? If so this would make the tree pre-Saxon – perhaps incorporated from a Celtic tree cult. However, who is to say that the Saxon vault was skewed to avoid a tree, and that the tree was this particular yew?

Best to fall back on Alan Mitchell's rule of thumb. It looks 1,000 years old. Probably it is older. The Celts may have decorated its branches with the heads of their victims. It may live to see our descendants flying to Mars. If awe-inspiring is too solemn a word, you might prefer 'wow'.

The Tandridge Yew

IN ABOUT 1745, AN IRISH SQUIRE, THOMAS PAKENHAM,

MY PREDECESSOR SEVEN GENERATIONS AGO AT

TULLYNALLY, OUR ESTATE IN WESTMEATH, PLANTED A

DOZEN SAPLINGS OF COMMON OAK (*QUERCUS ROBUR*)

IN HIS DEMESNE CLOSE TO THE MAIN DRIVE.

I can guess his motives. War, iron-smelting and a hungry population had stripped Ireland of most of its natural woodland in the preceding centuries. Now there was panic about the shortage of planking timber, especially oak, vital for building merchant ships and the fleet of the Royal Navy. By the 1740s, cash premiums were paid by the Irish Parliament to encourage the gentry to refurnish their estates with timber as a patriotic duty.

The Pakenhams, like most of the Irish gentry, were of English planter stock. So planting was something they understood. Besides, Thomas Pakenham had something to celebrate. He was moving up in the world. He had wooed and won the local heiress – Elizabeth Cuffe from Longford – worth £2,000 a year, with a borough in her pocket, and the prospect for her husband (if he voted for the Government) of a seat in the Privy Council and a barony.

THE SQUIRE'S WALKING STICK

The oaks, at any rate, grew tall and upright. Two hundred and thirty years after Thomas Pakenham, first Baron Longford, was laid in the family vault (and a century and a half after the British Navy turned with relief from wood to iron) these Tullynally oaks have reached their prime. Today the tallest of them, 109 feet to the top of its delicate green dome, is the tallest oak recorded in the Irish Republic. Height is not, however, its most remarkable feature. It is its eerie uprightness that makes it a prodigy.

It is almost exactly the same dimensions as the Duke of Portland's once famous oak at Welbeck, Nottingham, known as the 'Duke's Walking Stick'. This year, to celebrate the 250th anniversary of our ancestral walking stick, one of its offspring, five years old and seven feet high, has been planted in the National Botanic Gardens at Glasnevin, Dublin.

The Tullynally Oak

IN 1801 A YOUNG IRISH PEER, WILLIAM BURY, 2ND

EARL OF CHARLEVILLE, WAS FLUSH WITH

GOVERNMENT MONEY – COMPENSATION (OR A FAT

BRIBE, ACCORDING TO HIS ENEMIES) TO PAY FOR THE

LOSS OF HIS POCKET BOROUGH, SWEPT AWAY BY THE

ACT OF UNION. HE SPENT MOST OF THE CASH

BUILDING A FASHIONABLE NEW CASTLE AMONG THE

ANCIENT OAKS OF HIS DEMESNE NEAR TULLAMORE IN

KING'S COUNTY (NOW COUNTY OFFALY). IN

One branch on the right stretches 30 yards parallel to the ground

THE KING OAK OF KING'S COUNTY

DEFERENCE TO THE OAK TREES, HE

CALLED HIS HOUSE NOT CHARLEVILLE CASTLE BUT

CHARLEVILLE FOREST. ALREADY THERE WAS ONE

GIANT TREE KNOWN AS THE 'KING OAK'

DOMINATING, LIKE A WATCH TOWER, THE CARRIAGE

DRIVE TO THE TOWN.

Today the King Oak of Charleville is battered but unbowed, while the castle has lost its Arthurian grandeur, curtained off by an eccentric tenant behind a wall of breeze blocks. No one knows who planted the tree – king or peasant – or whether it sowed itself. But it seems to be a descendant of the great forests of common oak (*Quercus robur*) that once straddled the soggy green plains of central Ireland. Estimates of its age begin at 400 years; it might be double that. With a girth of 26 feet below its lowest branches, it is one of the oldest, largest and best-preserved oaks in the country.

Look at the span of its gigantic arms. One branch on the right of the photograph stretches 30 yards parallel to the ground. The Bury family believed that if a branch fell, one of the Burys would die, so they supported the great arms with wooden props. Of course there was nothing they could do to protect the trunk. In May 1963 a thunderbolt splintered the main trunk from top to bottom. The tree survived, but the head of the family, Colonel Charles Howard-Bury, dropped dead a few weeks later.

The Charleville Oak

BEECHES ON BORROWED TIME

A FEW MINUTES WALK DOWN THE GRASSY SLOPE TO THE

SOUTH OF OUR ANCESTRAL WALKING STICK, YOU WILL

FIND TWO OLD BEECHES VERY DIFFERENT IN SHAPE

BOTH FROM THE OAK AND FROM EACH OTHER.

The first is the epitome of the handsome parkland beech (*left*). Its trunk rises like a tower of smooth grey stone; its branches fall like the spray of a fountain. The second beech (*right*) is a pollard: squat, almost toad-like in appearance. In its youth the trunk was mutilated by pollarding to provide poles for the estate. Now its branches serve for trunks, coupling and recoupling in grotesque confusion.

Both trees are champions. By an odd chance, they share precisely the same girth measurement (22 feet 3 inches) which makes them the largest-girthed beeches in Britain or Ireland. And both are living on borrowed time.

When God made the beech, if botanists will forgive the expression, he made an architectural masterpiece, joining in one design the strongest form with the most delicate detail. Yet somehow he forgot to put in the foundations. Notorious for its shallow roots, the beech rarely lives more than 200 years. Even young trees, solid timber from top to toe, can be skittled over by a puff of wind.

Both these veterans in our demesne must be 18th-century trees. Their roots, judging by their capacity to feed a perfect dome of young leaves, seem sound enough. But I wouldn't wish to bet on it. There is an ominous void in their lower trunks. However, like most old beeches, they still preserve the smooth skin of their youth – irresistible to lovers and poets. As Andrew Marvell, the 17th-century metaphysical poet, confessed in *The Garden*:

> No white nor red was ever seen
> So am'rous as this lovely green.
> Fond lovers, cruel as their Flame,
> Cut in these Trees their Mistress name.
> Little, Alas, they know or heed,
> How far these beauties hers exceed!
> Fair trees! Where s'eer your barkes I wound,
> No name shall but your own be found.

I shall resolutely defend my beech trees from lovers and poets.

IN ARCADIA

THE TIMOUROUS HARE AND THE SPORTIVE SQUIRREL GAMBOL AROUND ME LIKE ADAM IN PARADISE,

BEFORE HE HAD AN EVE; BUT I THINK HE DID NOT USE TO READ VIRGIL, AS I COMMONLY DO HERE.

Thomas Gray on the joys of reclining under a beech at Burnham Beeches,
letter to Horace Walpole, Sept 1737. (from D. C. Tovey, *Letters of Thomas Gray*, 1900, I.7-8.).

RIGHT An ancient Scots Pine commanding the valley at Rothiemurchus with Ben Macdui beyond

RETURN OF THE NATIVES

ONE MISTY SEPTEMBER EVENING, MY EYE WAS CAUGHT BY THE PINK ROOTS

OF THIS ANCIENT SCOTS PINE. I WAS WANDERING IN YOUNG PINE WOODS

IN THE SPEY VALLEY, 50 MILES SOUTH OF INVERNESS.

The tree is not very large, or very old, in contrast to most trees chosen for this book. But its feet are enormous: a huge galumphing double layer of pink roots. It stands splay-footed among bushes of wild juniper on the side of a gravelly hill overlooking a small stream. From the size of its feet I would guess it to be about 200 years old. Wind and rain (and no doubt men, too, scooping out gravel for a track) have cut the ground from under it.

It is one of the last of the wild Scots pines of the great Caledonian Forest which, 2,000 years ago, was already the only place where native pines seem to have survived in Britain.

The largest remaining fragment of this forest is at Rothiemurchus, about 15 miles to the south. Here I photographed, a few months later, a pair of 200-year-old Scots pines at the meeting of two half-frozen tributaries of the Spey (I was wholly frozen myself). Beyond the two pines is a broad patch of heather and birch kept open by the deer; beyond the screen of young, self-sown pines rises the king of the Cairngorms, Ben Macdui, at 4,500 feet Britain's second highest mountain (*see front endpaper*).

When these ancient pines were young, parts of the forest were as wild as the forests of central Europe. Travellers on the road to Inverness had to run the gauntlet of wolves as well as highwaymen. But in the lifetime of these trees the natural forest has shrunk to a shadow; the pines were floated down the Spey to make rafters for English roofs and planks for English ships; and overgrazing by sheep and deer prevented the forest regenerating naturally.

But the worst seems to be over. Commercial forestry, battening on the taxpayer, is now triumphant. Sheep and deer are being fenced out. A century ago it was 'up horn, down corn'. Now it is 'up pine, down kine'. Best of all, the new forests include native trees as well as exotics, and not all the native pines are planted trees. Some landowners – including John Grant, the benevolent laird of Rothiemurchus – insist on allowing their pines to sow themselves.

Enthusiasts are even hoping to control the deer by restoring their natural enemy: the native wolf.

Before these ancient pines have finished scattering their cones in the heather, we may hear a pack of wolves howling at the moon over Ben Macdui.

Scots Pine in the Spey Valley

THE PIONEER OF ROTHIEMURCHUS

THE FOREST TREE THAT WE MOST TAKE FOR GRANTED IS THE

IRREPRESSIBLE COMMON BIRCH, EQUALLY AT HOME IN

MOUNTAIN, HEATH OR CAR PARK. TO BE PRECISE, MOST

BOTANISTS AGREE THERE ARE TWO COMMON BIRCH TREES,

THE SILVER BIRCH, *BETULA PENDULA,* AND THE DOWNY

BIRCH, *BETULA PUBESCENS,* BUT THERE ARE COUNTLESS

INTERMEDIATES.

What gave the birch a head start in the scramble to recolonize Britain and Ireland after the ice sheet melted was its powder-fine, wind-sown seed. No other common tree can produce an annual crop of a million seeds, each of which can travel miles on the wind to pioneer a new settlement.

I stumbled on the veteran shown here in a clearing at Rothiemurchus, a mile or two beyond the pair of ancient Scots pines at the meeting of the waters. Pine and birch make natural allies at the start of a new wood, although the pines eventually kill their allies by outshading them. However, this birch has exploited the clearing in the pine wood kept open by the deer. I should guess it is over a century old. Its bark, once silver, has been mottled and corrugated with age as if scraped by ice (and there was ice aplenty the day I saw it). Yet the envelope is unbroken, a mesh of delicate twigs ready to inflate into a balloon of pale green leaves.

Looking at this long-suffering solitary tree squatting by the river, it is easy to forget how fast birch can move if the situation demands. If the Scots abandoned Scotland to nature, it would be the birch that would be the first tree to seize its chance, and a birch forest that would walk the streets of Edinburgh.

Common birch at Rothiemurchus

VERY REVEREND VEGETABLES AT BURNHAM

A FEW MILES WEST OF HEATHROW AIRPORT, THE LAND-HUNGRY SUBURBS ARE

SUDDENLY BLOCKED BY AN ANCIENT COMMON, BURNHAM BEECHES. AS ITS NAME

SUGGESTS, IT HAS ALWAYS BEEN RATHER MORE THAN A COMMON, A MIXTURE OF

HEATHER AND GRASS, OF SCATTERED BIRCH AND THORN, AND OF ANCIENT OAK AND

BEECH FOREST, JEALOUSLY GUARDED BY THE CITY OF LONDON.

A mutilated oak, apparently medieval, survives on the western border. Nearby are ancient pollard beeches. It is unexpectedly arcadian. When the poet Thomas Gray lived nearby in the 1730s, he described the common as 'a little chaos of mountains and precipices' (of course he was exaggerating, the tallest mountain is a mound in a gravel pit 50 feet deep). He went on: 'Both vale and hill are covered with most venerable beeches and other very reverend vegetables, that like most other ancient people are always dreaming out their stories to the winds...' He would spend the whole morning 'growing to the trunk' as he put it.

Gray's beech is no longer visible (though he gave it immortality by moving it to Stoke Poges, five miles away, for his *Elegy Written in a Country Churchyard*). But one morning last autumn I photographed some of the descendants of Gray's reverend vegetables. They have the innocent air of trees that have planted themselves. In fact botanists believe that the beeches here, like those in other ancient beech woods of southern England, are descendants of the original beeches that came here after the last Ice Age ended 12,000 years ago. So behind the mask of innocence is a pre-Stone Age will to survive.

Beeches at Burnham Beeches

PART TWO
TRAVELLERS

OUT OF EUROPE

AND OVERHEAD UP GREW

INSUPERABLE HEIGHT OF LOFTIEST SHADE

CEDAR, AND PINE, AND FIR, AND BRANCHING PALM...

Milton's description of the exotic trees
surrounding the Garden of Eden in *Paradise Lost* Book IV.

PREVIOUS PAGE Cedar of Lebanon at Nymans
RIGHT The Mother Tree at Dunkeld drawn by J. G. Strutt in 1825

Larches at Dunkeld

DUNKELD'S MOTHER OF MILLIONS

ENGRAVED BY JACOB STRUTT IN 1825, WHEN THEY WERE

ONLY 70 YEARS OLD, THE LARCHES AT DUNKELD NEAR

PERTH WERE ALREADY THE MOST FAMOUS IN BRITAIN.

YOU CAN SEE THEM IN STRUTT'S ELEGANT ENGRAVING

(PAGE 41): ON THE LEFT THE RUINED CATHEDRAL OF

DUNKELD, ON THE RIGHT TWO OF THE LARCHES

PLANTED THERE BY THE LOCAL LANDOWNER, THE 2ND

DUKE OF ATHOLL.

Now compare them with the scene today, which I photographed during a blizzard in February 1996, enlivened by the noise of snow-heavy branches snapping in the wood behind my head.

The great larch, sole survivor of the five larches planted 250 years ago, throws out its arms theatrically, dominating the oak on the right and the cathedral behind.

It is known as the Mother Tree. When it came as a seedling packed in a basket brought in the stagecoach from London (more than a century after it first arrived in England) larches were almost unknown in the region. The Duke, the largest landowner in Perthshire, decided it was perfect for Scotland. In less than 20 years the first cones were being collected and the seeds sown. Before the 4th Duke died he was credited with planting 27 million larches on the barren hillsides around Dunkeld.

Few philanthropists have ever made such a radical transformation of a landscape, turning poverty to prosperity with a single idea. The tree grew fat where a sheep would have starved. The timber was so durable – unlike pine or spruce – that it could be used to build the hulls of boats. And what seemed just as important to aesthetes, it had the good manners to shed its needles in winter. Who could resist this new kind of conifer: pale green in spring, yellow in autumn, a skeleton in winter?

The larch was indeed perfect for Scotland. As it comes from the mountains of central Europe, it likes the rain-soaked scree of the hillside. Protected from the wind in steep Alpine valleys, it can grow huge and live for centuries. Experts claim that there are three larches at Ultental in the Alps that are 2,200 years old. (The claim is based on a ring count of a third tree supposedly taken in the 1930s.)

I do not expect the Mother Tree to live 2,200 years. But it should see us all out – peasants and Dukes alike.

The larch at Dunkeld

GROWING A NEW HEAD AT STRONE

THE COMMON SILVER FIR (*ABIES ALBA*), COMES FROM THE ALPS AND PYRENEES AND IS EUROPE'S TALLEST NATIVE TREE. NO ONE KNOWS WHO INTRODUCED IT TO BRITAIN, BUT IT WAS IMPORTED IN ABOUT 1600. SOON ITS HARSH, BRISTLY SILHOUETTE – REMINDING ONE ONLY TOO OFTEN OF A LAVATORY BRUSH – BEGAN TO BREAK THE SOFT, GREEN, BILLOWY SKY-LINES OF ENGLISH OAKWOODS AND BEECHWOODS. BUT CLOSE-UP, THE TREE, LIKE MOST CONIFERS, CAN LOOK BEAUTIFUL IN A COARSE KIND OF WAY. ITS TRUNK IS SILVER-GREY, ITS SPIKY NEEDLES GLOSSY AND DARK GREEN ABOVE, SILVER STRIPED BELOW.

The silver fir at Strone, Argyll has long been admired for its vast bulk and grotesque appearance. When it was young, about the time of the 1745 Jacobite rebellion, someone (no doubt an Englishman) beheaded it. The tree was irrepressible. All of its ten upper branches became trunks, sweeping upwards like ten huge, chubby, moss-covered fingers. By contrast its toes are quite delicate, modestly concealed in a ferny bank.

John Noble, the present laird of Strone, is understandably proud of his pet giant. (He has another Jacobite, a great beech called 'Bonnie Prince Charlie', which is supposed to have sheltered the rebels during the '45.) He sells a postcard claiming that this silver fir is the largest-girthed conifer in Europe. The tree has been officially recorded at a girth of 31 feet.

When it was measured in 1881 the girth was already over 15 feet, and the height about 100 feet. At that time it had 26 large companions: an avenue of silver firs planted to conduct the gentry down to the castle nearby. However Strone faces Lough Fyne, in one of the wettest and windiest corners of Scotland. No wonder most of the 18th-century silver firs have turned up their toes. But the survivor, John Noble's giant, is now dominated by a different species of silver fir, a grand fir (*Abies grandis*) from America planted by one of his ancestors in the 19th century.

Grand firs can far outstrip the common silver fir in height. For 20 years this grand fir was the supreme champion, the tallest tree in Britain and Ireland.

Sad to say, the grand fir lost its top in a storm a couple of years ago. It is now a mere 200 feet high – 12 less than the great Douglas fir at the Hermitage, Dunkeld (see page 50). But never underrate a silver fir. Like its companion beheaded in 1745, I should think it will calmly grow another head.

The silver fir at Strone

THE BEST AND THE WORST OF LIMES

HUNDREDS OF YEARS AGO THE TWO LIMES NATIVE TO

BRITAIN, THE SMALL-LEAVED LIME AND THE LARGE-

LEAVED LIME, FORMED A NATURAL HYBRID WHICH WE

NOW CALL THE COMMON LIME (*TILA X VULGARIS*). THE

HAPPY UNION OCCURRED IN BOTH BRITAIN AND

EUROPE. LIKE MANY OFFSPRING OF CHANCE

ENCOUNTERS, THE NEW LIME HAD HYBRID VIGOUR,

MEANING THAT IT GREW FASTER THAN EITHER OF ITS

PARENTS. IT WAS ALSO VERY EASY TO CLONE FROM

SUCKER SHOOTS.

By the 17th century it was fashionable to plant limes in Britain. Mass production by cloning made it the most formal of trees – especially if it was pleached or pruned. Its vigorous geometry suited the new landscape of walks and avenues radiating across Europe after the model of Versailles.

The Holker lime is probably a survivor from a formal layout of the early 18th century, when a great house was built here by the Lowther family. Later the estate was inherited by the brother of the 4th Duke of Devonshire to form one of the string of Cavendish palaces. Today the tree belongs to his descendant Lord Cavendish who has given it the freedom of the garden.

It is typical of the best – and the worst – of limes. Its girth inspires awe: 26 feet, and an official British champion, though its bloated shanks distort the measurements. Ten feet up, the grey bole vanishes into a tangle of whiskers, emerging as a dozen separate trunks. In June the tree forms a bower of the palest green. The air is heavy with the scent of lime flowers, humming with invisible bees. Less poetic is the shower of greenfly effluent ('honeydew' is too kind a word) that rains down from every vigorous common lime in July.

At Holker the great lime has its lower whiskers neatly clipped by a gardener. Many limes in British parks are not so fortunate. It seems that the clone that is common in Britain was a particularly whiskery one. In Europe the common limes are smooth-cheeked by comparison.

Perhaps there is a lesson. Bring in a better clone from the continent. Or plant one of the parents – smooth-cheeked, too, and far too fastidious to grow greenfly in their hair.

The Holker Lime

AMERICAN GIANTS

BEING UNABLE TO CLIMB OR HEW DOWN ANY [PINE CONES], I TOOK MY GUN AND WAS BUSY

CLIPPING THEM FROM BRANCHES WITH BALL, WHEN EIGHT INDIANS CAME AT THE REPORT

OF MY GUN. THEY WERE ALL PAINTED WITH READ EARTH, ARMED WITH BOWS, ARROWS,

SPEARS OF BONE AND FLINT KNIVES AND SEEMED TO ME ANYTHING BUT FRIENDLY..., I WAS

DETERMINED TO FIGHT FOR MY LIFE..., STOOD EIGHT OR TEN MINUTES LOOKING AT THEM

AND THEY AT ME WITHOUT A WORD PASSING, TILL ONE AT LAST, WHO SEEMED TO BE THE

LEADER, MADE A SIGN FOR TOBACCO WHICH I SAID THEY SHOULD GET ON THE CONDITION

OF GOING AND FETCHING ME PINE CONES...

From the journal of David Douglas, 26 October 1826, describing his
discovery of the Sugar pine near the Umpqua river, Oregon.

RIGHT Douglas fir at the Hermitage, tallest tree in Britain, in February 1996

OSSIAN'S DOUGLAS FIR

'AND THAT', SAID THE FOREST RANGER TO THE

SCEPTICAL TOURISTS, 'IS BRITAIN'S TALLEST TREE.'

We were looking across the pool, below the waterfall at the Hermitage, Dunkeld, facing a tall, young, elegant, arrow-headed Douglas fir. It seemed absurd: this young tree was 212 feet high, the tallest yet recorded in Britain. Only when the ranger scrambled down to the rocks by the pool did we have any grasp of the scale. This giant from North America is twice the height of most tall trees in Britain, and still going like Jack's beanstalk.

The two names for the tree – in Latin *Pseudotsuga menziesii*, in English Douglas fir – commemorate the men who described it and introduced it respectively. Archibald Menzies was the Scottish surgeon-naturalist on board one of Captain George Vancouver's ship, *Discovery*, sent by the British admiralty to survey the Pacific north-west in the 1790s. David Douglas was the young Scottish botanist sent out 30 years later to explore the interior and hunt for new trees and other plants. In due course Douglas introduced the grand fir and the sitka spruce, the two other giants from North America that compete for the honour of being Britain's tallest tree.

But the Hermitage tree is so young, and so well sheltered beside the pool, that it could keep its lead for many years. Forest Enterprise (formerly the Forestry Commission) actually own the tree; they do not bother to signpost it, and have no idea how old it is. My guess is that it is about a century old. In its home in Oregon or Vancouver Island, a Douglas will take three centuries to grow to 300 feet. The Hermitage tree might make that height a lot sooner.

How to convince Forest Enterprise that it is worth waiting?

Fifty yards from the tree is the Hermitage itself, a folly built in the 18th century by the Duke of Atholl to display to tourists the gigantic waterfall on the river Braan. Originally it was called 'Ossian's Hall'. Tourists were ushered into a dark room and shown a dimly lit painting of Ossian, the Gaelic warrior and poet (later exposed as a literary spoof written by a Scottish MP, James Macpherson). Then Ossian sprang back into the wall – and the tourists gasped at the raging waterfall almost under their feet.

Come back, Ossian. All is forgiven. We need you to celebrate a gigantic Douglas fir.

The Douglas fir at the Hermitage

THE REDWOODS OF WHITFIELD

LIKE SO MANY OTHER PACIFIC GIANTS, THE COASTAL REDWOOD (*SEQUOIA SEMPERVIRENS*) WAS SPOTTED BY ARCHIBALD MENZIES WHILE HE WAS SHIP'S SURGEON ON VANCOUVER'S EXPEDITION. (THE 'DISCOVERER', A FEW YEARS EARLIER, WAS THADDEUS HAENKE.) THE TOWERING RED TREES WITH SPONGY BARK GREW CLOSE TO THE SEA, A MERE 15 MILES FROM SAN FRANCISCO, AND STRETCHED ALONG THE WEST SIDE OF THE COASTAL RANGE AS FAR NORTH AS WHAT WAS TO BECOME THE STATE OF OREGON.

The new genus was given the name of the half-caste American Indian, Sequoya, who had invented the first Indian alphabet. But it was many years before the amazing facts about the new genus reached botanists, let alone the public.

It was the skyscraper tree, the tallest tree in the world, taller than all the other giants of the Pacific, taller than the eucalypts of Australia or the tropical hardwoods of Asia and Africa.

It was also magnificent lumber for the burgeoning cities of the west and the hungry railroads. No one knows how many thousands of ancient trees were logged before the loggers were finally brought to heel by the conservationists. There was, fortunately, one consolation. When cut down, the coastal redwood, unique among conifers, has the ability to bounce back. A new tree grows from the old stump. So there are now millions of young redwoods growing in the coastal ranges devastated by the first wave of lumber companies. Meanwhile, the first seeds had reached England in 1843 where they caused hardly a stir (it was to be different a few years later when a second kind of redwood, *Sequoiadendron giganteum* alias the Wellingtonia, was discovered; gardeners caught Wellingtonia fever). The new tree seemed choosy about soil and climate. Often it grew large but was bronzed by wind and frost, so that fine specimens were rare. Even rarer was a healthy grove of sequoias like the one at Whitfield, Herefordshire that I have chosen for my photograph (*see right*). These incongruous giants were planted by the Reverend Archer Clive in 1851.

Clive was a distant cousin of Clive of India; his hobbies included dendrology. There are now 20 redwoods in Archer Clive's grove and they are the biggest in any group in Britain. The tallest is 148 feet high, a pygmy no doubt in comparison with the 366-feet-high redwood, the 'Howard Libbey' tree in Humboldt State Park, the tallest tree in the world. But these are early days yet.

To stand among the redwoods of Whitfield, with the early morning sun clipping their spongy red trunks and brilliant green foliage, is to sniff the Pacific air that Menzies breathed 200 years ago.

Lime Avenue

WELLINGTONIAS:
NEW GIANTS FOR OLD

THE MOST SENSATIONAL DISCOVERY IN THE

MOUNTAINS OF CALIFORNIA WAS THE DISCOVERY OF

SEQUOIADENDRON GIGANTEUM, KNOWN HERE AS THE

WELLINGTONIA AND IN THE UNITED STATES AS THE

GIANT SEQUOIA OR BIG TREE.

The Gardeners Chronicle splashed their scoop across the front page on Christmas Eve 1853. A new giant had been tracked down in California by a British plant explorer. It was to be named *Wellingtonia gigantea* in homage to Britain's hero, the Duke of Wellington, who had died the previous year.

Wellingtonia mania swept the country a year later when the first seedlings were put on sale in Britain (they were also on sale in Europe and the east coast of America). One-year-old seedlings were two guineas each and snapped up in thousands. The trees grew two feet a year shaped like green rockets. They were planted everywhere: on suburban lawns, on great estates, in triumphal avenues. The tallest, a tree at Castle Leod, Highland is now 174 feet high.

Strange to say, it was never fashionable to plant them in groves. The trees in my photograph are a striking exception: a grove of 14 Wellingtonias now 130 feet high. They were planted by Holford at Westonbirt in the 1860s. When I visited them in July 1995 there was a heatwave and the mercury touched 91°F. The smell of resin was overpowering.

By the 1860s Wellingtonia mania was beginning to subside. It had been ingeniously promoted by the Exeter firm of Veitch; and what a stroke of genius to associate the new giant with the old giant Britain had just lost. Veitch had sent out a Cornish plant explorer, William Lobb, to hunt for botanical treasures in California. Lobb arrived in San Francisco at the height of the gold rush. In the summer of 1853 he heard rumours that a grove of giants had been found by a gold miner in the Sierras, 200 miles south-east of the city.

It turned out that the discoverer was a hunter called A.T. Dowd. One day he was pursuing a wounded grizzly bear in Calaveras County when he stumbled into a grove of extraordinary trees. He returned to camp and told his companions, who thought him drunk or dreaming. Then they, too, stared awestruck upwards. There were 80 or 90 trees up to 300 feet high, and several girthed 70 feet. They proved the largest living organisms on Earth.

Lobb wasted no time in hiring horses to go to Calaveras County. He filled his pockets with seed, took cuttings and even dug up two small plants. Then he returned to England as fast as a sailing boat could carry him round Cape Horn. This was a triumph for himself – and a gold-mine for Veitch.

LEFT AND BELOW The Wellingtonia Grove at Westonbirt

MONEY-MAKERS OF SCONE

SITKA SPRUCE GETS A BAD PRESS THESE DAYS. THEY

HAVE DARKENED THE FACE OF THE FLOW COUNTRY IN

NORTHERN SCOTLAND WITH THEIR SHAPELESS

FORESTS. ONLY FORESTERS LOVE THEM FOR THE MONEY

THEY MAKE. IF YOU WANT TO MAKE MONEY IN

WESTERN BRITAIN OR IN IRELAND, PUT IT IN SITKA.

Yet the young trees are pushy, spiky, ill-tempered brutes with blue-green needles apparently made of barbed wire. The old trees are martyrs to greenfly, which somehow munch through those terrible needles, leaving the branches thin and mangy. Tell a good gardener that you are planting a specimen tree of Sitka and he will smirk. Yet look at this pair in the Scone Palace arboretum outside Perth. They are both champions: at 20 feet in girth the largest yet recorded. And who could fail to admire the grey flaking bark and the deeply fluted trunks which give a whiff of the Oregon rain forests to the suburbs of Perth?

This was David Douglas' third great introduction after his travels of 1827-8. At first the economic importance was not recognized. Foresters in Britain are cautious – and perhaps it is just as well. For 100 years after Douglas' death, foresters played safe by planting the old faithfuls from Europe – common spruce (the so-called Christmas tree) and European larch – and re-introducing from the Caledonian Forest our native Scots pine.

Then the penny dropped. The Sitka's miraculous talent was discovered. It seemed to convert rain into wood with no need for much soil in the process. You could plant it in shallow peat above a bog, or scatter it over a rush-strewn hillside. Then it could rain cats and dogs every day for a year. The Sitka revelled in it. In 40 years you could get your money back with interest, compared with 60 years for common spruce and a century for Scots pine.

On poor, wet, western soils the Sitka is king. On good soils it has only one commercial rival: the Douglas fir.

At Scone arboretum you can compare both rivals viewed as specimen trees, and I must admit there is no comparison. With its dark green foliage, hanging like tassels, and its wonderful corky brown bark, the Douglas gets my vote. At Scone there is a special pathos about all Douglas' introductions. This was the garden where he worked as a boy, and to Scone he sent back packets of seed from the original Douglas firs in Oregon. Tragically, he died aged 35, mangled by a wild bull in a pit-trap in Hawaii, before any of his giants had grown bigger than a bush.

Two champion sitka spruce at Scone

THE TREE THAT LONGS TO GET AWAY FROM HOME

YOU WOULD THINK THAT ALL TREES ARE HAPPIEST AND GROW BEST AT HOME. BUT THE MONTEREY CYPRESS GROWS BETTER ALMOST ANYWHERE ELSE. I CAN CERTAINLY SYMPATHIZE. HOME FOR THIS CYPRESS IS THE ROCKY COAST OF MONTEREY BAY, ONLY AN HOUR'S DRIVE SOUTH OF SAN FRANCISCO.

It is one of the most beautiful places in the world – unless you are a tree. They have rocks at their feet and the wind from the Pacific blows straight in their faces.

All the original natives whose ancestors survived the last Ice Age – only a few hundred trees – live in Monterey Bay or an even less hospitable island nearby. No wonder these natives are stunted and gnarled: a lesson for travellers who take the wrong turning. Some palaeobotanists believe that the tree got lost on its way back from Central America after the ice sheet melted. The other giants of the Pacific – the Douglas fir, the Sitka spruce, the grand fir and so on – returned safely to their homes in the deep soils of the Rockies and the coastal mountains of the north-west. The Monterey Cypress somehow turned left and went off on its own.

However, life has changed for the tree since it was brought to Britain and Europe (and of course other parts of North America) in about 1838. Of all the true cypresses that can put up with our so-called temperate climate, the Monterey Cypress grows fastest, is healthiest and becomes biggest.

This one at Montacute House, Somerset, is about 125 feet high, nearly twice the height of the tallest survivor at Monterey. It is little more than 140 years old and is still growing. Often these trees age badly; the dark green skirts of their youth turn to thickets of naked branches. However, the National Trust own this tree and are proud of it. Tree surgeons have kept it looking almost youthful, manicuring its long bony arms and shaving its rugged trunk.

Recently the Monterey Cypress has been losing ground as a fashionable tree, supplanted by its bastard offspring, the Leyland Cypress. This intergeneric freak – a cross between a true cypress (*Cupressus macrocarpa*) and a false cypress (*Chamaeocyparis nootkatensis*) – grows faster and is tougher than either parent. It will make a 30-feet-high hedge in a dozen years. But as an ornamental tree I think it will prove a disappointment.

A woman, men used to say in France, needs to suffer to be beautiful. Perhaps a tree is the same. The years of exile have added nobility to the aura of the Monterey. The Leyland is an upstart: smooth, green, characterless, smug.

The Monterey Cypress at Montacute

IMAGINE A TALL TREE WITH UNEARTHLY FOLIAGE AND 5,000 TULIPS IN ITS HAIR. IT SOUNDS LIKE A PRE-RAPHAELITE

PAINTING. BUT THE TULIP TREE (*LIRIODENDRON TULIPIFERA*), IMPORTED FROM NORTH AMERICA, GIVES REALITY TO

THE VISION.

TULIPS
A HUNDRED
FEET
HIGH

In the south of England, a tree like this veteran at Kew forms a flower bed 110 feet high. Before they open fully, the tubes of pale green petals, flecked with orange, look uncannily like green tulips (in chilly Scotland and Ireland the flowers are hard to find).

Equally surreal is the foliage. Each malachite-green leaf, picked out with a rim of yellow, has been sliced off at the end – truncate-retuse to the botanist, more like a heraldic emblem to the rest of us.

John Tradescant the younger, gardener to Charles I, apparently brought back this trophy to Britain after a series of journeys in eastern America in the mid-17th century. Over there the tree was regarded with awe, but not because of its flowers. Under the name of Yellow Poplar, the tree could grow to a height of 170 feet in the deep farming soils of Kentucky and Virginia, head and shoulders above all other hardwoods (except the Western Plane, there called sycamore). The pioneers used them for canoe wood. It was in the trunk of a tulip tree, a hollowed out log about 60 feet long, that Daniel Boone packed his family and belongings and set off for Spanish territory.

In the cooler summers of Britain the tree rarely exceeds 100 feet. But who knows? Global warming may do the trick. At least it might make the tree flower properly in my garden in Ireland.

LEFT AND ABOVE The tulip tree at Kew

FROM THE EAST

IN THE MIDST OF THIS PLAIN ARE THE CEDARS OF WHICH HOLY SCRIPTURE MAKES MENTION WHICH ARE

IN NUMBER TWENTY-TWO STANDING, WHERE THEY SAY TO HAVE BEEN SINCE THE CREATION OF THE

WORLD, AND THAT GOD TRANSPLANTED THEM... AND IF IT BE OBJECTED THAT THE DELUGE HAVING

INUNDATED THE WHOLE EARTH COULD NOT HAVE SPARED THIS PLACE, SINCE IT EVEN DESTROYED THE

EARTHLY PARADISE, AND CAUSED ALL PLANTS TO DIE, EVEN THE TREE OF LIFE, IT IS TRUE; BUT THE

CEDARS BEING ENDOWED BY GOD WITH A GUMMY QUALITY, THIS GUM...PRESERVED [THEM] IN THE

UNIVERSAL INUNDATION.

Fr. Eugene Roger's description of the Cedars of Lebanon in *La Terre Sainte* (Paris, 1646).

RIGHT The Goodwood Cedar of Lebanon planted in 1761

STORM-BATTERED CEDARS OF LEBANON

NO LATER PASSION FOR EXOTIC TREES, NOT EVEN THE

VICTORIANS' LUST FOR WELLINGTONIAS AND MONKEY

PUZZLES, QUITE EQUALLED THE FRISSON CREATED BY

THE CEDAR OF LEBANON.

Its origins were at first mysterious. When the seeds reached London in the mid-17th century, no one knew which traveller had brought them from the East, nor whether they would survive our wetter climate. But the credentials proved unimpeachable. This was the great cedar of the Bible, the tree of Solomon's temple, which had somehow clung to life in a few scattered groves in the mists of Mount Lebanon.

No wonder the fashionable world crowded round the four specimens planted in the Physic Garden at Chelsea by Sir Hans Sloane. Perhaps there were scoffers. But the trees grew, and in turn withstood the hurricane of 1703, the great frost of 1740, the hurricane of the 1770s. By the end of the 18th century they were sizeable creatures, overshadowing the glasshouses (two of the four had to be cut down for that reason).

Meanwhile, almost everyone who was anyone planted one in his park, adding to the sober evergreens of Europe – silver fir, spruce, larch and pine – the spicy flavour of the East. But many failed. The home of the tree is in the rocks and scree of Mount Lebanon (and, as it later turned out, it flourishes on an enormous scale in the high rocky valleys of the Taurus Mountains of Turkey). In the rich soils of Britain the tree grew too fast for its own good. Most of the 17th-century trees (but not those at Chelsea) had died before the next century was out. Two-hundred-year-old trees are rare, usually battered out of recognition by storms.

Two of the biggest survivors can be found in Sussex. The cedar at Goodwood was planted in 1761, and lost half its six heads in the hurricane of October '87. The cedar of Nymans was probably planted in about 1800. The hurricane nearly demolished it. Only the cosmetic skills of the National Trust have restored its appearance. But it is a raddled beauty on the lawn at Nymans. Soon it will be dead.

In the spring of 1993 I visited the valley in the Taurus Mountains where what are the reputedly the oldest cedars grow. Most of them are smaller than our trees, and they do not have their elegance. They are gnarled and tormented trees, up to 1,000 years old. In the hot wind we could smell the resinous tang of Solomon's temple.

The Nymans cedar half demolished

by the hurricane of '87

PICK A STRAWBERRY

THE STRAWBERRY TREE (*ARBUTUS UNEDO*) HAS ONE

DISTINCTION THAT APPEALS TO THE IRISH. APART FROM

A DUBIOUS SPECIES OF WHITEBEAM, IT IS THE ONLY

SPECIES OF TREE NATIVE TO IRELAND THAT HAS

TURNED ITS BACK ON BRITAIN. COMING FROM THE

MEDITERRANEAN, IT TOOK THE SHORT CUT FROM

BRITTANY AFTER THE LAST ICE AGE, UNLIKE THE REST

OF IRELAND'S NATIVE TREES WHICH PLODDED ALONG

VIA DOVER AND HOLYHEAD.

Its flowers hang in clusters of white bells, rather like heather; in fact they both belong to the same family, the *Ericaceae*. Its fruit look delicious. Like small strawberries they make a striking spectacle in November. You will not try eating them more than once. (Hence the Latin name, *unedo*, which is supposed to be an abbreviation for 'I only eat one'.) As an antidote to the plague, however, we are assured by the 17th-century herbalist, John Pechey, that the flowers and fruit make an excellent concoction.

Although it grows wild in three counties of western Ireland, sharing the rocky shores of the Killarney lakes with oaks, yews and ferns, the common arbutus is often no more than a bush. More exotic and tree-like is the hybrid arbutus from Greece that I photographed one glowing February evening at Kew. This is the hybrid called *Arbutus x andrachnoides*. It occurs naturally in Greece and Turkey where the two species of arbutus, *unedo* and *andrachne*, grow side by side among the rock roses and the wild thyme.

At Kew they have added a Greek temple to make it feel at home (or perhaps it was the other way round). The tree is about 35 feet high: huge for a strawberry tree. Its bark is bright cinnamon – unlike the grey-brown of the wild Irish tree – peeling to violet and yellow. But, be warned: its flowers and fruit are disappointing.

If you need an antidote to the plague, you had better pick your strawberries from an arbutus in Killarney.

The hybrid strawberry tree at Kew

XERXES' PLANE AT EMMANUEL

HANDEL'S ONLY COMIC OPERA, *SERSE*, OPENS WITH THE

HERO, XERXES, SITTING UNDER A LARGE PLANE TREE

SINGING:

> *Ombra mai fu*
> *di vegetabile*
> *cara ed amabile*
> *soave piu*
>
> (No shade is more sweet
> Than the shade
> Of this dear and lovable
> Vegetable.)

The opera sank into well-deserved obscurity itself, but Handel rescued the tune and recycled it as his famous *Largo*.

He took the story of Xerxes and the plane tree from Herodotus. The great king of Persia was marching to Sardis when he encountered a magnificent plane tree at Kallatebos near the crossing of the River Maeander. So delighted was he with its shade that he loaded it with golden ornaments and arranged for a man to stay there as its guardian forever.

'What good did it do the tree?' asked a 3rd-century author, a killjoy called Aelian. The great king had made a fool of himself, losing his heart to a tree, hanging bangles on it and setting a guard over it as though it were a lady of his harem.

The Fellows of Emmanuel College, Cambridge do not share Aelian's puritanical sentiments. They have indulged their pet oriental plane (*see left*) with half an acre of the Fellows' Garden, and guard the tree as uxoriously as did Xerxes.

Although still young – certainly not planted before 1802 – the tree has covered the lawn with its curtain of zig-zag branches, that sweep down to form 'layers', then rise again as new trees in their own right.

In southern England this species of plane, *Platanus orientalis*, grows quite as fast as in Greece or Turkey. But it is rare in comparison with the hybrid plane, the so-called London plane, *Platanus x hispanica*. The oriental plane has more beautiful leaves, as they are cut into more elegant lobes, but the hybrid plane is the workaday tree for towns and cities; more upright, and more stoical in dealing with buses, it is better suited to life in the pavement.

At Emmanuel, at any rate, the oriental plane is in clover. Not that Xerxes himself is honoured there. As the invader of Greece, he is the villain of classical studies; in fact he was marching to invade Greece when he encountered the plane tree. Fortunately the Persians got their deserts at the battle of Thermopylae. Indeed this tree at Emmanuel could be said to celebrate the victory of democracy and the downfall of the Persians. For, in 1802, some seeds from a plane tree were brought home from Greece by a Cambridge don, Daniel Clarke, and one of them was apparently planted at Emmanuel. He collected the seeds on the battlefield of Thermopylae.

HOOKER'S CHOICE AT KEW

THERE ARE 600 SPECIES OF OAK IN THE WORLD, ABOUT 100 OF WHICH CAN MUDDLE THROUGH IN OUR WAYWARD CLIMATE. IF I HAD TO CHOOSE ONE FOR MY DESERT ISLAND IT WOULD BE THE CHESTNUT-LEAVED OAK (*QUERCUS CASTANEIFOLIA*) FROM THE MOUNTAINS OF IRAN. AND IF I COULD TAKE A FULLY GROWN ONE WITH ME I WOULD CHOOSE THIS TREE AT KEW, REPUTED TO BE THE FINEST THIS SIDE OF THE CASPIAN.

The tree makes one dizzy with superlatives. It was planted in about 1846, the first in Britain. It is still unchallenged champion. Sir William Hooker, had just begun to impose his will on Kew – and on the British government who financed it. Of all the thousands of trees and shrubs he ordered to be planted in his years as director, this tree became the most enduring symbol. It is the biggest tree in the gardens, 120 feet tall and over 23 feet in girth, and seems to revel in Kew's notoriously frugal soil. Yet it is so finely proportioned that you could pass it without any idea of its bulk.

I photographed it one morning in May, when the crinkly, sweet chestnut-shaped leaves had begun to unfurl, but the architecture was still unobscured. The elephant-grey trunk divides at about 30 feet into a kind of irregular vault which in turn supports an immense dome. Judging by the rakish profile, the tree is still putting on height fast. But the hurricane of October '87 which devastated Kew must have hit this tree like a battering ram. I counted the scars from a dozen big limbs lost recently. Some wounds were unhealed. A fungus was making its home just under the vault.

Do not rely on this colossus keeping its fine proportions for ever. Often the trees that grow fastest die first. Unless you plan a trip to the Caspian next week, take a bus to Kew.

The chestnut-leaved oak at Kew

MAPLES AS PINK AS A SHRIMP

I DROVE TO WESTONBIRT, THE ARBORETUM IN GLOUCESTERSHIRE, ONE MISTY MORNING IN OCTOBER 1994. THE PARKLAND WAS FULL OF PARKED CARS. 'IS THERE A POP CONCERT, OR CAR RALLY?' I ASKED WITH DISMAY, 'NO, THEY'VE COME LIKE YOU – TO SEE THE MAPLES.'

He was perfectly right. I had come to see the maples, reputedly the finest collection this side of Mount Fujiyama, and so had 2,000 others, alerted to their autumn splendour by Westward TV. There are more kinds of Japanese maples at Westonbirt than all the tree species in my garden, perhaps 200 different varieties. Sir George Holford, who owned this arboretum at the turn of the century, bred maples as other men breed pigs or racehorses. Their colours in autumn extend sunset for three solid weeks – ranging from shrimp-pink to kimono-scarlet, from mutton-red to yellow-fever yellow.

The current owners, Forest Enterprise, keep up the good work, replacing Holford's derelicts (a Japanese maple is usually worn out by the time it is 60) with young plants the colour of coral.

The first Japanese maple reached England in about 1820, by way of China, long before Japan was opened up to foreigners. The species, *Acer palmatum*, had been secretly drawn and described 45 years earlier by a Swedish doctor-botanist, Carl Pieter Thunberg, a disciple of Linnaeus. He was employed by the Dutch East India Company at their trading post near Nagasaki. And there he was supposed to stay, confined to an artificial rocky island a quarter of a mile across. However, Thunberg was a man of resource, and the only European doctor for a thousand miles. Once a year he was allowed to join a caravan for Edo, the imperial capital, in order to treat the ailments of the Emperor and the Court. On the journey he collected plants, drawing them as though they were medical specimens.

If you ever feel sated with maples the colour of shrimps or coral, try and find one of the original species, as depicted by Thunberg. Judging by the theatrical stance of the branches, and the cut of the green leaves, it is the largest and the most elegant. It is also the longest living. I found a huge one once on a hillside in County Donegal, deserted like Madame Butterfly by Pinkerton.

LEFT AND RIGHT

The Japanese maples at Westonbirt

MYSTERIOUS MOTHERS

'ABOUT 80 OR 100 YEARS AGO AS FAR AS I CAN MAKE OUT A TENANT

ON THIS ESTATE FOUND TWO YOUNG YEWS GROWING ON THE

MOUNTAINS NEAR BENAUGHLIN...FROM THE ONE BROUGHT TO

FLORENCE COURT ALL THE PLANTS NOW IN EXISTENCE ORIGINATED.'

3rd Earl of Enniskillen to Francis Whitla (21 December 1841).

RIGHT The Florence Court Yew, mother of all Irish yews in the world

SOLEMN AND UPRIGHT AT FLORENCE COURT

ACROSS A MUDDY FIELD, HALF A MILE FROM FLORENCE COURT, COUNTY FERMANAGH – THE 18TH-CENTURY HOUSE THE FIRST OWNER LOVINGLY NAMED AFTER HIS WIFE – IS THE ORIGINAL IRISH (OR FLORENCE COURT) YEW (*SEE LEFT*).

Its progeny (*Taxus baccata* 'Fastigiata'), all ultimately descended from cuttings taken from this one tree in Ireland, now people the world in millions. No other mutation of tree has achieved this feat of multiplication. Its dark, solemn, upright descendants have travelled from Europe to the Antipodes, and to both sides of the Rockies – where they are especially welcome in graveyards. A new richness has been added to the Irish persona, not normally associated with uprightness and solemnity. How did this miracle occur?

Dr Charles Nelson, the former taxonomist at the National Botanic Gardens, Dublin has explored the site and explained the miracle.

In about 1760 one of the tenants of Lord Enniskillen who had inherited the estate – a farmer called Willis – found a rum-looking pair of yews growing wild in the Cuilceagh Mountains above Florence Court. He planted one at home, and gave the other to Lord Enniskillen, who planted it there in the demesne. In due course the tenant's died, but the landlord's flourished, and began to attract attention because of its unusual uprightness. By the early 19th century the Florence Court Yew was well known to enthusiasts, and a commercial nursery had begun to sell cuttings under that name.

Poor Mr Willis. If he had patented the tree he would have made his fortune. But it was impossible then – and is still difficult today – to patent a cultivated variety of tree.

If you cross the muddy field at Florence Court to pay your respects to the mother of millions, do not expect very much. The Northern Ireland Ministry of Agriculture own the tree, and have cut back the laurels and ash trees; there is a metal plaque to inspire you. But, strange to say, the tree that has put Ireland on the map is a poor specimen of its own type. Only its upper branches look upright at all. It is *Taxus baccata* 'Semi-fastigiata' these days. Could one say, if you will forgive the pun, that 230 years of being solemn and upright have overtaxed the *taxus*.

The original Irish yew at Florence Court

BASTARDS ARE BEST AT BRYANSTON

ANYONE WHO MEASURES THE HEIGHT OF THESE TWO LONDON PLANES (*PLATANUS X HISPANICA*) AT BRYANSTON,

DORSET WILL ASSUME EITHER HE, OR HIS HYPSOMETER, HAS GONE BARMY. BUT HE WILL BE WRONG. THESE ARE

BRITAIN'S TWO TALLEST HARDWOODS, 152 AND 158 FEET HIGH RESPECTIVELY, TOWERING OVER ALL THE BEECH, OAK,

LIME, ASH AND OTHER CHAMPION HARDWOODS IN THESE ISLANDS.

And both have trunks to match, girthing 16 and 18 feet, giving them such graceful proportions that they rise effortlessly from the ferny track, as though there was nothing in this achievement, and British woods were stuffed as full of trees 160 feet high as a tropical rain forest.

In fact they represent the triumph of hybrid vigour, of the principle that bastards are best.

The London plane, as we saw, is believed to be a cross between the oriental (Greek and Turkish) plane and the western (American) plane. But how and where the union occurred is a mystery. Some scholars claim that the chance encounter occurred in the garden of John Tradescant the younger in Lambeth. Tradescant, Charles I's gardener, visited eastern America three times in the mid-17th century, and we know that he reared American planes side by side with his Greek ones. But to hybridize, both species would have had to flower – unlikely to have happened so soon. Besides, the American plane cannot tolerate our damp climate and soon goes into a decline, suffering leaf wilt.

Much as one would like to believe the story of stolen kisses in Tradescant's garden, it is more likely the union occurred, prosaically, somewhere in Spain (hence the current name, *hispanica*). However, Tradescant did give away young planes to his friends, and no doubt helped to make the bastard fashionable.

In the last 300 years it has taken the urban world by storm. Every square in central London, every fine boulevard in Paris, in fact most cities in temperate climates from Ireland to western China, are bursting with London planes. They are the most long-suffering creatures imaginable. But of course they prefer a peaceful life in a warm climate.

These giants at Bryanston School have made their home just where one would expect to find them: half-forgotten beside a ferny track, with rich, damp soil at their feet, not too far from the sea, with a hill between them and the wind, and only the odd jogger to ruffle the leaves on the forest floor.

The champion London planes at Bryanston

CHINOISERIE

THEIR ARTISTS DISTINGUISH THREE DIFFERENT SPECIES OF SCENES,

TO WHICH THEY GIVE THE APPELATIONS OF PLEASING, HORRID AND

ENCHANTED... THEY INTRODUCE INTO THESE [ENCHANTED]

SCENES ALL KINDS OF EXTRAORDINARY TREES...

Sir William Chambers on the Art of Laying out gardens among the Chinese, 1757.

RIGHT Bark of Kew Ginkgo showing 'chi-chi'

GOING DOWNHILL FOR 60 MILLION YEARS

TO COMPARE THE GINKGO FAMILY WITH SOME ARISTO-CRATIC FAMILY FROM CENTRAL EUROPE, WHO HAVE BEEN GOING STEADILY DOWNHILL SINCE THE MIDDLE AGES, HARDLY DOES JUSTICE TO THE GINKGO FAMILY.

They have been going downhill ever since Tertiary times, 60 million years ago. In fact the lineage of this tree, *Ginkgo biloba*, makes the dinosaur look like an upstart. The family became powerful 350 million years ago, before the Alps and the Himalayas were a gleam in the Creator's eye; the tree took an early form 150 million years ago, before the first pterodactyl had hatched in its nest up a tree fern.

That is why botanists give this one tree the unique honour of one species, one genus, one family and one order, all for itself.

With such a pedigree, the ginkgo might be expected to look somewhat fossilized (and in a literal sense it does). But this fine specimen at Kew (*see left*), first to be famous in Britain and still one of the biggest there, is healthy enough. That it came from China you might suspect from its irregular cascade of branches, and its nobbly grey-brown trunk with breast-like protuberances called 'chi-chis'. But the leaf shaped like a butterfly would baffle you. There is no rib bisecting it. It reminds one of a maidenhair fern (and 'Maidenhair tree' is the English name). Of course, this is the clue. When ancestral ginkgos were making their way in the world 350 million years ago, there were no other trees, only ferns.

This specimen arrived at Kew in 1762 by way of a Thames barge; it spent the first few years of its life at the Duke of Argyll's estate at Whitton, then Lord Bute moved it to Kew for the Dowager Princess of Wales' new arboretum. He also transplanted a Chinese pagoda tree (*Sophora japonica*), which survives today, a stretcher case, recumbent on steel crutches. Sir William Chambers had already been commissioned to build a ten-storey pagoda nearby which made Chinoiserie all the rage.

To keep up with the times, 18th-century gentlemen planted ginkgos in their pleasure grounds. But the tree has a drawback. Although it is almost extinct in the wild, its last natural home was in south-east China, where they have hot summers. So it turns up its nose at most parts of Ireland or Scotland. But it is happy in the stockbroker belt of the Home Counties. It also enjoys life in the gardens of Buddhist temples in China, Japan and Korea and in the pavements of Washington DC.

At home in China it might live 1,000 years or more. Here it will grow faster and die sooner. But its ancient lineage gives it one advantage. It evolved long before any leaf-eating insect existed.

So the insects that mutilate the leaves of other trees – oaks, beeches and so on – cannot touch a hair on the ginkgo's head.

IN 1899 A YOUNG ENGLISH HORTICULTURALIST, ERNEST WILSON, WAS OFFERED £200 BY THE FIRM OF VEITCH TO GO

TO CHINA AND BRING BACK SEEDS OF WHAT WE NOW CALL *DAVIDIA INVOLUCRATA*, THE HANDKERCHIEF TREE OR

DOVE TREE.

TO LAUGH OR TO CRY
AT ROWALLANE

The new species had been discovered in 1869 by Père Armand David, the celebrated French missionary and naturalist (who also gave his name to a species of deer). He had made elegant drawings of the tree showing its ghostly white bracts that hang down like white handkerchiefs (or like doves, if you prefer). But no one, it seemed, had yet introduced the plant to Europe or America.

Veitch were the leading British nurserymen of the period, and could afford to pay several thousand pounds for a packet of seeds with such spectacular commercial prospects. The trouble was that Père David was dead, and so perhaps was the *Davidia* he had discovered in Sichuan. No one could be certain. An Irish doctor and plant-hunter, Augustine Henry, was said to have seen one somewhere. So Veitch's order to Wilson was: to find the *Davidia*, you must first find Augustine Henry.

A year later Wilson tracked Henry down in the jungle close to the Indo-China border with China. Henry gave him a sketch-map of the village where he had seen a *Davidia* 20 years before. Eight months later, after a roundabout trip by way of Hanoi, Shanghai, and the Yangtse gorges, Wilson reached the village. He heard the sound of chopping. And there was Henry's tree, cut down for roof beams.

A lesser man would have thrown in the towel – or wept into his own handkerchief. Wilson gritted his teeth and plodded off to look in the direction of Père David's tree, further north. After a few weeks he found several, and they were flowering. In 1900 Wilson wrote back in triumph to Veitch enclosing a packet of large seeds like walnuts, the long-awaited *Davidia*.

Then the blow fell. And was Wilson to laugh or to cry? Unknown to the British, the French had won the race five years earlier. In 1897, one of David's successors, Père Farges, had sent *Davidia* seeds to Vilmorin's nursery in Les Barres, France. There were 37 seeds in the packet, and only one germinated. But it grew rapidly and first flowered in 1906, five years before Wilson's seedlings. This is the mother tree of one variant (called *Davidia involucrata vilmoriniana* because its leaves are smoother underneath) from which most of the handkerchief trees in the world have been propagated.

My photograph shows the tree at Rowallane, County Down – an early introduction from Farges' seed. The tree lost its main trunk soon after planting. It is a glorious bush, 50 feet high and 50 feet wide, and every May it produces enough handkerchiefs to blow a thousand noses or dry a thousand pairs of eyes.

The handkerchief tree at Rowallane

TRY PLANTING A HIMALAYAN MAGNOLIA TREE AND

THEN WAIT 30 YEARS FOR IT TO FLOWER. THE

EXCITEMENT IS TERRIFIC.

EGRETS OR FLAMINGOS?

I was given a plant in 1979 by a generous magnolia breeder, Julian Williams, the owner of Caerhays Castle, Cornwall. His family have been magnolia-mad and camellia-mad for three generations (his father created the famous 'Williamsii' hybrid camellias in the 1930s). He introduced me to the brother of my new plant, the tree in this photograph; the mother tree was the original immigrant from Himalaya.

This tree at Caerhays is the white variant of Campbell's magnolia, relatively rare in cultivation, although this is the common type of the wild species that roams in Himalaya from Nepal to China. At present this is only a youngster of 50 feet, but in its prime it could double that. Already it produces 1,000 flowers every spring, each eight to ten inches long. In early April the tree looks as though it was home to a flock of white egrets.

The two best-known magnolias native to North America – the evergreen *Magnolia grandiflora* and the deciduous *Magnolia macrophylla* – both flower in summer. These deciduous Asiatic ones flower in early spring before the leaves have returned. It is this, and the enormous size of the flowers, and the towering height of the tree that makes it worth waiting half a lifetime for Campbell's magnolia to reach maturity.

By the way, I did not have to wait 30 years for my own plant to flower. It produced two flowers last year, 18 years from seed. The flowers are the size of soup bowls and an amazing colour. Julian Williams had warned me not to expect pure white. They are actually pink, the colour of old-fashioned ladies' underwear.

But I am delighted. I shall not have a flock of egrets in my garden. I shall have flamingos.

Fig. 1

Campbell's magnolia at Caerhays

A WHIFF OF THE JUNGLE

WE WERE IN A WORLD OF FERN-TREES, SOME PALM-LIKE AND OF

GIGANTIC SIZE, OTHERS QUITE JUVENILE; SOME TALL AND ERECT AS

THE COLUMNS OF A TEMPLE, OTHERS BENDING INTO AN ARCH, OR

SPRINGING UP IN DIVERGENT GROUPS, LEANING IN ALL

DIRECTIONS...

Mrs Meredith (an early settler in Tasmania) on giant tree ferns,
from *My Home in Tasmania* (1852) II. 161-164

The sea at Rossdohan, Co. Kerry, blue as the tree ferns

PARADISE REGAINED AT HELIGAN

THE EERIEST GARDEN IN CORNWALL, HELIGAN NEAR

TRURO, CALLS ITSELF THE 'LOST GARDEN OF HELIGAN',

AND THIS NOT JUST A REFERENCE TO THE MADDENING

SIGNPOSTS. THIS IS A LOST WORLD OF SORTS. THE TREE

FERNS PRESENT THE SPECTACLE OF A PRIMEVAL FOREST

IN THE GEOLOGICAL AGE OF 100-FEET-HIGH

CLUBMOSSES AND HORSETAILS. IT IS AS IF ONE HAD

STUMBLED BACK IN GEOLOGICAL TIME TO THE HEROIC

ERA BEFORE FLOWERING PLANTS – BEFORE EVEN THE

GINKGO.

Heligan was also lost for many years in the sense that its owners fled, and left the plants to their own devices. Some plants enjoyed the freedom. But an understorey of *Rhododendron ponticum*, originally brought in to shelter the weak, took a terrible toll. Fortunately, a charitable trust was set up to save Heligan from itself. The trust has worked wonders. Many ancient trees have been rescued alive, including the tree ferns.

You can see three examples of the common tree fern, *Dicksonia antarctica*, behind the wishing well in this photograph. Two are alive; the centre one has been killed (presumably by *ponticum*). The 15-feet high trunks are one of the plants' specialities. Botanically they are ferns not trees. This is not a real trunk, conducting nutrients from roots to leaves. It is just a 'caudex': a pile of old roots and decaying fronds on which the fern is perched and through which its living roots must penetrate.

Most spectacular of all are the fronds. Every year a *Dicksonia* can produce 30 new fronds six feet long, arching like those of a palm tree. You feel warmer when you look at a *Dicksonia*. But the species comes from the cool, wet mountains of Australia. It shuns sunlight. All it asks is for a daily bucket of cold water over its head.

Cornwall is happy to oblige. And you can use a tree fern for an umbrella.

Common tree ferns at Heligan

TREE FERNS
AS BLUE
AS THE SEA

COLLECTORS' TREES OFTEN LOOK DULL ENOUGH TO

THE REST OF US. BUT HERE IS A RARITY THAT WOULD

CAPTURE THE IMAGINATION OF A STONE. IT IS THE

CYATHEA DEALBATA, A NOTORIOUSLY DELICATE TREE

FERN FROM NEW ZEALAND, GROWING AT ROSSDOHAN

IN THE WILDS OF COUNTY KERRY.

There are hundreds of *Cyatheas* in this garden where frost probably finds it harder to penetrate than anywhere else on the mainland of Britain or Ireland. At any rate these are the only *Cyatheas* known to be frisking about in the open and spreading like weeds, up here at latitude 51°, 30' North, except for some immigrants to the Scilly Isles.

Like the *Dicksonia*, the *Cyathea* needs to keep wet to keep healthy. But it is altogether more elegant. The trunk is tall and sinuous like that of a cocoa nut palm. The fronds are blue-green, silver underneath and arch their backs like ostrich feathers.

This specimen crouches in a jungle of other ferns, under the wing of a towering *Eucalyptus globulus*. I photographed it on a morning of tropical brilliance in early October 1994. They had told us the evening before, when we were at Kenmare, further from the open sea, that frost was almost unknown in this happy land. Next morning the fields were white with hoar frost right down to the shore of the estuary. At Rossdohan there was no hint of that. The garden was carved at the end of the 19th century out of a small rocky island, warmed by the waters of the bay, and the ramparts of Bishop pine are now in their prime.

When they breed a new *Cyathea* in New Zealand as tough as old boots (which means tough enough for my garden) my cup will overflow.

Blue tree ferns at Rossdohan

PART THREE

SHRINES

SACRED TREES

THEREFORE, WITH RESOLUTION AS HIS ONLY SUPPORT AND

COMPANION, HE SET HIS MIND ON ENLIGHTENMENT AND

PROCEEDED TO THE ROOT OF A PIPAL TREE [BO-TREE], WHERE THE

GROUND WAS CARPETED WITH GREEN GRASS.

Prince Buddha finds enlightenment under a Bo-tree.
From the *Life of Buddha* (edited by Avril de Silva-Vigier).

PREVIOUS PAGES Wordsworth's yews at Borrowdale;
three survive from the 'Fraternal Four'
RIGHT Inside the yew at Much Marcle

GLOOM
OR
BLOOM
AT
MUCH MARCLE

The seasons bring the flower again,
And bring the firstling of the flock,
And in the dusk of thee, the clock
Beats out the little lives of men.

O, not for thee the glow, the bloom,
Who changest not in any gale,
Nor branding summer suns avail
To touch thy thousand years of gloom.

Alfred Tennyson, *In Memoriam,* Stanza II

The yew at Much Marcle, Herefordshire, is one of about 50 gargantuan yews found in British churchyards, that is, yews of more than 30 feet in circumference. Hence it is presumed to be at least 1,000 years old, like the yew of Tennyson's *In Memoriam.* It is 31 feet at the base, bottle-shaped, and completely hollow for the first ten feet. It probably pre-dates the Christian church built there in the 13th century.

Once its branches might have carried pagan trophies, or the severed heads of sacrificial victims. Christianity would have purged it of that. Until the Reformation, its dark green leaves would have provided 'palms' for the Palm Sunday procession; before the introduction of exotics from Europe, no other suitable evergreen would have been available. (The word 'palm' is still used as a synonym for yew in some parts of Britain.)

As a Christian symbol the tree faced two ways like Janus' head. Life was the meaning of the tree that seemed itself immortal. Death was the meaning of the poisonous, scarlet berries and the tough pink wood, as springy as steel, used for spears, arrows, bows.

In these respects the yew of Much Marcle is typical of its contemporaries. Yet, despite Tennyson's hard words, I found it a cheerful tree. The huge canopy of branches, supported on cast iron columns, acts as an extension of the south porch. The hollow interior of the main trunk has been fitted up with a bench for parishioners, as though it was a garden pavilion.

To be fair to Tennyson, he thought better of the 'thousand years of gloom'. In a revised version the stanza reads:

To thee too comes the golden hour
When flower is feeling after flower.

The Much Marcle Yew

Where they used to come with me together,

Ten hundred angels were there

Above our heads, side close to side.

Dear to me is that yew tree:

Would that I were set in its place there.

From the 16th-century *Life of St Columcille* by
Maurice O'Donnell (translated from the Irish).

AMONG THE ANGELS AT MUCKROSS

We know from the medieval Welsh priest, Geraldus Cambrensis, that yews were favourites in Ireland. He paid four visits to the country soon after its invasion by the Normans in 1172. 'Yews', he writes in his *History and Topography of Ireland*, 'are more frequently to be found in this country than in any other I have visited; but you will find them principally in old cemeteries and sacred places, where they were planted in ancient times by the hands of holy men, to give them what ornament and beauty they could.'

Today, eight troubled centuries later, ancient yews in churchyards are much rarer in Ireland than in England or Wales. But at Muckross Abbey, near Killarney, County Kerry, there is a famous specimen in the centre of the ruined cloister.

It was first described in the *Tour of Ireland* written by Arthur Young, the English agricultural improver, who visited Ireland in 1776 looking, often in vain, for landlords who shared his ideas. The *Tour* is heavy going. On his way back to London, Young rashly gave his trunk, containing his private journal, to a servant at Bath who walked off with it. So the book is stronger on turnip yields than on picturesque anecdotes. But he mentions the yew of Muckross with awe and delight: 'without exception the most prodigious yew I ever saw.'

One is tempted to say that Young knew more about turnips than yews. For the Muckross yew was only two feet in diameter, as he says. And that is only a snip for a yew – even in Ireland.

However there are two things prodigious about the Muckross yew: its elegant shape and its strange position. It grows at the precise centre of the cloister of the Franciscan abbey, its red-brown trunk rising like a corkscrew, its stubby branches radiating like an umbrella.

Is it a wild yew that sowed itself there before the Franciscans arrived? Or was it planted by them for some purpose after the cloister was built?

The locals believe that the yew came to Muckross before the men of God. I would like to share their faith. But when you look at its size and its well-pruned shape, it appears to be a planted tree. I would expect it was planted some time between the foundation of the abbey in the 15th century and its dissolution at the Reformation in the 16th century. If so, it was put there to give 'ornament and beauty' (in the words of Geraldus) and also no doubt to provide palms for the Palm Sunday procession, like all old yews planted beside churches. Of course it was probably a wild yew once – a willing captive, so to speak, taken and transplanted and tamed by the Franciscans, as they tamed the birds and the beasts. (It looks even more like a captive today, as the Office of Public Works, who manage the ruins, have caged the yew to protect it from tourists.)

Only a mile from Muckross are the celebrated yews of Killarney, the largest wild wood of yews in Ireland, a wood as black as a monk's cowl. This is a place to delight St Columcille himself – with enough yews for ten thousand angels to sit on, side close to side – and it grows on a bony outcrop of limestone that came from the sea millions of years before.

The Muckross Yew

POETS' TREES

...A YEW TREE WHICH IS THE PATRIARCH OF YEW TREES, GROWING AND

FLOURISHING, IN VERY OLD AGE – THE LARGEST TREE I EVER SAW. WE

HAVE VERY LARGE ONES IN THIS COUNTRY, BUT I HAVE NEVER YET SEEN

ONE THAT WOULD NOT BE BUT AS A BRANCH OF THIS.

Dorothy Wordsworth, on the Lorton Yew, *Letters*, 7 and 10 October 1804.

RIGHT The path to Wordsworth's yews at Borrowdale

WORDSWORTH'S YEWS AT LORTON AND BORROWDALE

There is a yew, the pride of Lorton's vale,
Which to this day stands single in the midst
Of its own darkness as it stood of yore ...
Of vast circumference and gloom profound
This solitary tree! – a living thing
Produced too slowly ever to decay;
Of form and aspect too magnificent
To be destroyed.

Wordsworth, *Yew Trees*.

'Is anything left of Wordsworth's tree today?', I asked my host in the neat, white-washed village of Lorton in the Lake District, and was shown a young yew tree that was not born when Wordsworth wrote *Yew Trees* in 1803. I thought that was that.

Then I stayed in Lorton again a year or two later. I peered behind a derelict brewery – and rubbed my eyes. Could it be...? Great heavens, it was. Half hidden behind the wall, on the edge of the Hope Beck (*see left*), unknown apparently to any of the men of Lorton, was the Pride of Lorton's Vale.

It was solitary to this day, as Wordsworth said – gaunt against the misty fields below the rocks of Hobcarton Crag. But, strange for a romantic poet, Wordsworth had forgotten the power of the wind. Half the tree had been torn off by a storm in the 19th century, reducing the size of the trunk to a mere 13 feet. The local farmer's sheep were paying homage to the surviving half of the trunk by eating off a ring of bark.

Here was a 1,000-year-old tree famous long before Wordsworth. Fox the Quaker evangelist preached to a crowd overflowing into its branches. Did anyone care about it today? I drove to Cockermouth, three miles away, to see the Mayor's chair made from the wood. It was marked 'Wordworth's Tree'. But the lady who showed it me had no idea the tree was alive and well and growing new branches.

South of Hobcarton Crag, and beyond Keswick, is the wild valley of Borrowdale also made famous by Wordsworth in *Yew Trees*:

But worthier still of note
Are the fraternal four of Borrodale
Joined in one solemn and capacious grove;
Huge trunks! ... ghostly shapes
May meet at noontide ...
   there to celebrate
As in a natural temple scattered o'er
With altars undisturbed with mossy stone
United worship ...

The 'fraternal four' lost one of their number in the great storm of 1883. Otherwise the yews still look much as Wordsworth described them. This is a holy spot. It is rare for great yews to survive on a bare hillside, away from the shelter of park or graveyard. Sadly, I had the feeling, as I did at Lorton, that no one particularly cares for these famous trees. The National Trust owns the hillside, but has left the trees to their own devices – and the homage of the sheep.

THE TREE THAT DID NOT GO TO DUNSINANE

I will not be afraid of death and bane
Till Birnam forest come to Dunsinane.

Shakespeare, *Macbeth,* Act V, Scene III.

Macbeth was misled by the witches, as every schoolboy knows. Birnam wood did go to Dunsinane, with the boughs camouflaging Malcolm's soldiers, and Macbeth got his just deserts. But here is an oak tree that Shakespeare would have known if he had gone up there to do his research. Somehow it stayed behind in Birnam.

It looks medieval: the last of the great oak forest that once straddled the banks and hillside of the River Tay a mile east of Dunkeld.

I photographed it on a suitably wild day in February 1996, taking refuge, at the height of the snow storm, in the hollow trunk. (I can't recommend this in normal circumstances, as other occupants use the tree for a different purpose.)

The tree's far-flung arms are propped on eight wooden crutches, and it looks remarkably fit, considering it is hollow for the first ten feet of the trunk.

Congratulations to the local tree support group. Most authorities would have said that Macbeth's tree was dangerous, and removed its head – like Macbeth's.

Macbeth's oak at Birnam

Sidney's oak: today a burnt-out ruin

COMMEMORATING A WAR HERO

ACROSS THE PARK FROM PENSHURST, THE SIDNEYS' GREAT

HOUSE IN KENT, IS A TREE CALLED 'SIDNEY'S OAK', LONG

ASSOCIATED WITH SIR PHILIP, THE ELIZABETHAN WAR HERO

AND POET.

Recently, I was told, some children set fire to it and it is now a ruin. When Jacob Strutt drew it in 1822 (*see above*) it was already hollow and stag-headed, but still a huge tree, 30 feet in circumference.

Is this the oak that was famous because of the lines in Ben Jonson, claiming that it was planted at Sidney's birth in 1554?

That taller tree of which the nut was set
At his great birth where all the Muses met.

When John Claudius Loudon was writing his book on trees in the 1830s he asked the head of the Sidney family, Lord De L'Isle, to settle the question.

Lord De L'Isle replied that Ben Jonson (and later Edmund Waller) must have invented the story of the birthday oak. The tree

dated from the Middle Ages, and was the poet's favourite tree, the one under which he sat to write poems about shepherds and shepherdesses.

In February 1995 I went down to Penshurst to photograph the tree, taking a copy of Sidney's works. The page fell open at the lines about sheep from *Astrophel and Stella*:

Go, my flock, go get you hence
Seek a better place of feeding.

The tree certainly looked medieval. It had broken in half, then burnt out. And the Penshurst sheep were quietly eating what was left of it. I don't think the poet would have minded. At any rate, if his poems can be believed, he adored sheep.

TREES OF LIBERTY

O GLORIOUS FRANCE, THAT HAS BURST OUT SO; INTO UNIVERSAL

SOUND AND SMOKE; AND ATTAINED THE PHRYGIAN CAP OF LIBERTY.

IN ALL TOWNS, TREES OF LIBERTY ALSO MAY BE PLANTED;

Thomas Carlyle, *The French Revolution* (I.423).

The Tolpuddle Martyrs under the Sycamore tree, and the
government spy who reported them

MARTYRDOM AT TOLPUDDLE

ON THE VILLAGE GREEN AT TOLPUDDLE, DORSET, CLOSE

TO THE MARTYRS' INN, IS A VERY LARGE, MUTILATED

SYCAMORE. JUDGING BY THE HUGE BOLE OF FLAKING

PINK-BROWN-GREEN BARK, I WOULD GUESS IT TO BE 250

YEARS OLD, ONE OF THE OLDEST SYCAMORES IN

BRITAIN.

This is the Martyrs' Tree, and over the years it has been well cared for, perhaps too well: its head is shorn like a convict's, its trunk pinioned with rusty iron bands.

For this is a shrine and a place of pilgrimage for the Left. It was under this tree, in 1834, that six agricultural labourers, exploited by their employers, formed the first trades union in Britain. They wanted to bargain for better pay and conditions. They were arrested on the warrant of the local magistrate, sent to Dorchester for trial accused of sedition, found guilty, sentenced to seven years and transported to Botany Bay.

Nineteenth-century British society had its tensions, but not the seismic faults of Europe. The Tolpuddle Affair did not tear Britain apart (as France was to be torn apart by the Dreyfus Affair at the end of the century).

The plight of the six labourers – we would call them the Tolpuddle Six – was taken up in a dignified manner by the Opposition in Parliament. There were monster petitions and protest meetings, and broadsheets showing the six men sitting under the tree. Lord Liverpool's government was embarrassed: the sentence did seem somewhat steep. So back the Martyrs came, after three years as sheep-farmers in Australia, to live out their lives by the sycamore on the village green; and whatever you thought of them, they had certainly put Tolpuddle on the map.

I wish I could say this story had a happy ending – I mean the story of this remarkable tree. But I was shocked by the sight of its own martyrdom: the concrete choking its stomach, the iron rods cutting into its ancient bark.

Some martyrs really do suffer a fate worse than death.

The Martyrs' sycamore at Tolpuddle

Kett's Oak at Wymondham

THE ARCH-REBEL'S OAK

DURING THE FRENCH REVOLUTION THE TREE OF

LIBERTY WAS OFTEN AN OAK.

IN BRITAIN THE OAK HAS BEEN THE SYMBOL OF THE

MONARCHY EVER SINCE THE BOSCOBEL OAK RECEIVED

ITS APOTHEOSIS. IT HAD SAVED CHARLES II FROM

CAPTURE BY THE CROMWELLIANS. OAK DAY WAS

CELEBRATED ON 29 MAY, AND THE ROYAL OAK,

COMPLETE WITH A PICTURE OF THE KING UP A TREE,

BECAME A FAVOURITE PUB SIGN UP AND DOWN THE

COUNTRY.

The cult of the Boscobel Oak hastened its demise. Patriotic folk tore off branches to show their appreciation. It was dead by the end of the 19th century (although its descendant is there at Boscobel today).

But Kett's Oak at Wymondham, Norfolk has survived from a much earlier period, when an oak could be a symbol of revolution. Robert Kett was an unlikely leader for a peasant revolt. He was a 57-year-old tanner and substantial landowner at Wymondham, three hours walk from Norwich. In July 1549 he led an uprising against

the Crown. A mob of small-holders (drunk according to their enemies) had assembled under an old oak tree on the common outside the village. They demanded an end to the enclosure of common land. Kett, who had taken some himself, agreed with them. He made a rousing speech, and the mob marched off to Norwich, gathering strength as they went. Soon Kett's army numbered 20,000 and captured Norwich Castle. Kett drew up a list of 29 demands for the reform of abuses in Church and State. But King Edward VI wasn't interested in Kett's list. He sent the Earl of Warwick who easily crushed the revolt. Staves and pitchforks were no match for guns and cavalry. Kett was captured, condemned for treason and hanged at Norwich Castle.

But his spirit – and his oak tree – lived on.

Under the name of the Reformation Oak, the old oak tree outside Wymondham was a place of regular pilgrimage for radicals. John Evelyn, tree adviser and friend of Charles II, preferred oaks to all other trees. But this is how he described Kett's Oak in his famous *Sylva*:

> In the meantime I met with but one instance where this goodly tree has been (in our country) abused to cover impious designs, as was that Arch Rebel Kett, who, in the reign of Edward VI (becoming leader of the fanatic insurrection in Norfolk) made an Oak (under the specious name of Reformation Oak) council house, and place of convention where he sent forth his traitorous edicts.

No doubt Evelyn would have liked to chop the tree down with his own hands. He would grind his teeth if he knew that Kett's Oak is one of only three trees described in *Sylva* that survived the next 330 years intact. (There is also another Kett's Oak in Norfolk, at Ryston, but I am assuming that Evelyn was referring to the tree at Wymondham.) Its survival is all the odder because the tree is within an arm's length of the road to Norwich, now the B1172, but the same road that the doomed rebels marched down in 1549 (although the common has now been enclosed as fields of oil-seed rape).

Dodging cars and lorries, I photographed it in June 1994.

Kett's admirers put an iron fence round the tree 100 years ago, and later the local authority obliged with a prop and a lay-by. In 1953 a rapprochement with the Crown seemed likely. To mark the Coronation, one of Kett's acorns was planted nearby. But the Arch-Rebel was not to be reconciled. At any rate the acorn disappeared.

PART FOUR

FANTASIES

GATEWAYS & HOMES

THE INTERIOR IS HOLLOW AND HAS BEEN FITTED WITH A TABLE IN

THE CENTRE, AND BENCHES AROUND. THIS ROOF HOWEVER, AS IT

MAY BE TERMED, HAS FALLEN IN.

The Crowhust Yew described in Bayley's *History of Surrey* (1850) Vol. IV, 132.

PREVIOUS PAGE The 18th-century tree house in the broad-leaved lime at Pitchford Hall

RIGHT Looking into the heart of the yew at Crowhurst

ONE LOOKS AT AN ANCIENT YEW AS ONE MIGHT LOOK AT MEDIEVAL ARCHI-

TECTURE, MARVELLING AT THE INTRICACY OF THE CRAFTSMANSHIP IN WOOD.

BUT SOMETIMES THE LINE BETWEEN TREE AND BUILDING BECOMES BLURRED.

THE CAVE AT CROWHURST

A couple of miles from the great yew of Tandridge is a sister tree, of roughly the same girth (31 feet compared to 34 feet) but probably of even greater age. This is the yew at the west end of the churchyard at Crowhurst, Surrey.

It was cited by Evelyn in *Sylva* as one of the oldest trees he knew, and again by John Aubrey in his history of Surrey.

The trunk is completely hollow, leaving inside a space about six feet in diameter. Early in the 19th century it was apparently fitted out as a room, with tables and chairs. The conversion brought to light a cannon ball from the Civil War which had somehow embedded itself in the wall of the tree. On the east side of the room a doorway was cut and a wooden door attached.

Who made their home in the tree is not made clear. Was it a summer house for the vicar, or a gambling den for the sexton – or just a hole for the coal? A storm struck the tree in 1845 and brought down the roof. But the tree still had table and chairs inside when inspected by John Lowe, the yew expert, half a century later.

When I photographed it in July 1994, the door was ajar but no one was at home. The interior now presents a bizarre spectacle. New wood on an old yew tree accumulates like coral. The old room now resembles a cave glowing with pink fretted rock.

I shall recommend Crowhurst when I next meet a hermit looking for a home.

The Crowhurst Yew

TEA IN A TREE AT PITCHFORD

THE BROAD-LEAVED LIME (*TILIA PLATYPHYLLOS*) AT PITCHFORD HALL, NEAR SHREWSBURY, IS THE LARGEST IN GIRTH KNOWN IN BRITAIN OR IRELAND. WITH THE MASSIVE, GREY BRANCHES CHARACTERISTIC OF THE SPECIES, IT LOOKS AS THOUGH IT HAS BEEN A GIANT FOR CENTURIES. IN FACT THERE IS A MAP OF THE GARDEN DATING FROM THE END OF THE 17TH CENTURY: ALREADY THE TREE WAS BIG ENOUGH TO CARRY A HOUSE ON ITS HEAD.

That building may have been a simple garden hut in the tree. The present tree house dates from the mid-18th century, probably designed by Thomas Pritchard, a Shrewsbury architect.

The owners, the Ottley family, built and rebuilt their main house over the centuries (you can see the Jacobean chimneys on the lower right of the photograph). A hundred years ago the exterior of the tree house was stucco and the roof was slate. Later it was half-timbered and tiled to match the main house.

The tree itself was pollarded, and sheets of lead were wrapped over the hollow where the trunk joined the branches. In this state it has survived hurricanes without disaster. The Colthurst family were less fortunate. They joined Lloyd's as 'Names' – and were struck by a series of hurricanes. Pitchford had to be sold. The mysterious new owner (the locals claim he is an Arab) generously allowed me to see the tree house.

I climbed the wooden staircase and pushed open the door. There was room for chairs and a decent-sized tea table. It is said that Queen Victoria, who was god-daughter of one of the owners, took tea here as a young woman. The plasterwork is elegant: a delicious Rococo soufflé of Chinese, Gothic and Classical. This was the style made famous by Batty Langley in his book, *Ancient Architecture Restored*, published in 1742. But the lime tree upstages the plasterwork.

Outside, the eight-feet-thick branches throw monstrous shadows on the ogival window panes.

ABOVE The Pitchford broad-leaved lime

LEFT Interior of the tree house

A South East View of the Green Dale Oak near Welbeck.

The Greendale Oak in 1775

UNDER THE TREES AT WELBECK

THE GRANDEST DUKE, IN THE CORNER OF RUTLAND

AND NOTTINGHAM SO FULL OF STRAWBERRY LEAVES

THAT IT WAS CALLED THE DUKERIES, WAS THE DUKE OF

PORTLAND – AT LEAST IN THE 18TH CENTURY. THE 3RD

DUKE, PRIME MINISTER IN 1783, THEN HAD THE FINEST

PARK WITH THE MOST ANCIENT OAK TREES.

Two oaks stood guard at either side of the north gate; they were known as the Large Porter and the Little Porter. Their heights, measured by a tree enthusiast called Major Rooke in 1790, were 98 feet and 88 feet respectively.

A generation later, Loudon was informed by the 4th Duke's gardener, Mr Mearns, that both Porters had lost ten feet and were in decline. 'At some far distant period they have been spreading, lofty and noble trees... They are still grand in decay.'

Today the Little Porter has somehow been given a new lease of life (*see right*). It greets you on the left as you go down the drive towards the house, a burly, broad-shouldered tree that conceals its age – hardly less than 450 years if it was ancient in 1790 – behind a fresh green beard and mutton-chop whiskers. The Large Porter also

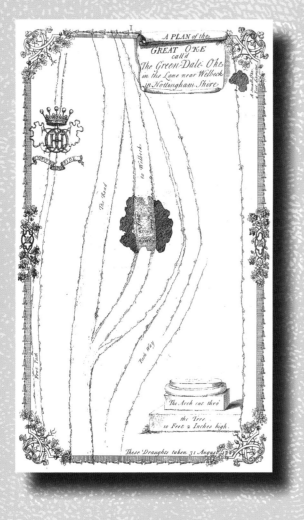

ABOVE AND RIGHT The Greendale Oak drawn by George Vertue in 1727

survived till recently; then a storm knocked it flat.

Much the most famous of all the Duke's trees was the Greendale Oak. The two Porters merely attended you as you drove through the gate; the Greendale Oak was a gateway in itself.

The story was told that in 1724 the 1st Duke told a friend at dinner that he had an oak tree so large that you could drive a coach and four horses through it. 'Will you bet on it?', asked the friend. The Duke gave orders to his woodmen. While the gentlemen lingered over their punch, the woodmen cut an archway in the tree, ten feet high and six feet wide. Next morning the Duke's narrowest carriage drove through the Greendale Oak and won him the wager.

The mutilated tree was measured, described and engraved like an anatomical specimen over the next 200 years, gradually diminishing in size, but still painfully recognizable.

During the later 19th century these great oaks at Welbeck passed unnoticed by their owner, the 5th Duke, styled the 'Mole Duke'.

He did not drive through the Greendale Oak. He drove underneath the trees in the park in a tunnel designed to carry him unseen by his neighbours (he was a shy man, the 5th Duke) to his private railway station.

The Greendale Oak drawn by J. G. Strutt in 1826

PILLARS OF ST EDWARD'S

MOST OF THE YOUNGER GENERATION OF YEW TREES CROUCH MEEKLY IN THE GRAVEYARD. THIS PAIR STAND LIKE PILLARS BY THE NORTH DOOR OF ST EDWARD'S, STOW-ON-THE-WOLD. I ADMIRE THEIR AUDACITY.

'They were considered a menace, and were going to be cut down', said the vicar, Mr Rothery. 'But they won't be touched in my time.' Bravely spoken, Mr Rothery.

By arrangement with Mr Rothery, I spent a happy afternoon on a step-ladder, pruning the whiskers from the tree on the right so that I could take a photograph.

I suppose they were planted some time in the 18th century to frame the north door. There must have been some kind of formal avenue. How else to explain the pink, ribbed trunks, bare and upright as far as the beginning of the lancet arch?

Now the roots are spreading like lions' paws, and toying with the Victorian boot-scraper.

I hope this will divert their attention from knocking down the church.

The twin yews at St Edward's

WALLS, WALKS & PUZZLES

NO PLEASING INTRICACIES INTERVENE,

NO ARTFUL WILDNESS TO PERPLEX THE SCENE.

GROVE NODS AT GROVE, EACH ALLEY HAS A BROTHER,

AND HALF THE PLATFORM JUST REFLECTS THE OTHER.

THE SUFFERING EYE INVERTED NATURE SEES –

TREES CUT TO STATUES: STATUES THICK AS TREES.

Alexander Pope, *Moral Essays.*

The Great Umbrellas at Levens Hall, survivors from the 17th century when the
garden was laid out by Guillaume Beaumont, formal gardener to James II

THE HEDGE THAT UPSTAGED EMMA THOMPSON

I would rather look upon a tree in all its luxuriance
and diffusion of boughs and branches, than when it is cut
and trimmed into mathematical figures.

Joseph Addison, in the *Spectator*, 1712

The fashion for formal gardening, for pleaching limes and hornbeams
and making topiary out of yew, ended in Britain soon after Addison
issued this romantic challenge in the *Spectator*. Within ten years
William Kent had made his famous highjump into landscape
gardening; in Horace Walpole's phrase, he 'leapt over the fence, and
saw that all nature was a garden'.

Most of the great British gardens built and planted in the
formal style in the preceding two centuries then succumbed to the
new craze for nature. No one uprooted more miles of fine yew hedges
and topiary with more iconoclastic zeal than Capability Brown. But a
few formal gardens escaped the onslaught of the improvers – or were
restored when formal gardens returned to fashion a century later.

Both processes – survival and revival – are represented in these
formal gardens at Levens Hall, Cumbria and Montacute, Somerset,
owned by the National Trust. You can see the original hedge in the
back of the photograph of Montacute. After three centuries of
clipping it has developed a surreal style of its own, breaking free from
the planned geometry. You can't miss its special style if you look at the
scenes in the film of *Sense and Sensibility*, shot in the garden at
Montacute; I thought the hedge upstaged Emma Thompson.

Hardly less extraordinary are the topiary eggs, clipped from
Irish yew, which supply the main theme of the restoration. I can only
show two eggs, but there seemed to be hundreds. Irish yew, whose
foliage is thicker, and more upright than common yew's, takes
clipping with even better grace. It is also always female – which means
it produces berries even when clipped. When I photographed
Montacute in the shimmering summer of 1995, each egg was glowing
with berries like scarlet buttons.

NOBLESSE OBLIGE AT MEIKLEOUR

THE GREAT BEECH HEDGE OF MEIKLEOUR IS JUSTLY

FAMOUS. TAYSIDE HONOURS IT WITH A SIGNPOST, THE

AUTOMOBILE ASSOCIATION WITH AN ENTRY IN THE

MAP. IT RUNS FOR A QUARTER OF A MILE ALONGSIDE

THE A93, THE MAIN ROAD FROM PERTH TO BRAEMAR: A

GREEN WALL OF BEECH PLANTS SET 18 INCHES APART

AND NOW 100 FEET HIGH.

It was apparently planted in about 1745 to give shelter to the big house at Meikleour, then belonging to the Nairne family. The story goes that the men who planted it were called away to fight in the Jacobite Rebellion, and not one of them returned alive from the Battle of Culloden.

To pay tribute to their memory the hedge was allowed to grow to the heavens.

I asked the present owner, the 8th Marquess of Lansdowne, who inherited the estate through a Nairne ancestor, whether the story was true. He is a handsome octogenarian, and passionate lover of trees. He welcomed me to his golf buggy. However, he snorted when I mentioned the great hedge of Meikleour. I could see I had raised a delicate subject.

Of course a hedge the height of a ten-storey building is no bed of roses. To prune it would need a crane or a scaffold; the men would take their lives in their hands; just consider the danger money.

'It's all tosh about the hedge', he said firmly.

Shame on you, Lord Lansdowne. Your ancestors fought and bled for King James.

But, wait, I had misinterpreted my host. What he meant was that he doubted the story, but he recognized his lofty responsibilities. He would go on spending a fortune pruning the monster.

The beech hedge at Meikleour

AN AVENUE OF PUZZLES AT BICTON

THE STORY GOES THAT IN 1795 ARCHIBALD MENZIES,

THE SURGEON ON BOARD CAPTAIN GEORGE

VANCOUVER'S SHIP *DISCOVERY,* EXPLORING THE PACIFIC,

WAS OFFERED NUTS FOR DESSERT AT A BANQUET GIVEN

BY THE PRESIDENT OF CHILE, AND POCKETED A

HANDFUL. THE SHIP HAD ANCHORED ON THE WEST

COAST OF CHILE, WHERE THESE NUTS WERE THE STAPLE

DIET OF THE ARACAUNOS INDIANS OF THE HIGH

ANDEAN PLATEAUX.

Menzies planted the nuts in flower pots and watched them grow into singular-looking pine trees. Instead of having needles, arranged in regular whorls (like spokes on a wheel), this pine had scale-like leaves arranged in spirals. The plant was christened '*Araucaria aracauna*' after the Indian tribe. Thirty years later, when Menzies' trees had grown into a spiky freaks, someone remarked: 'To climb that would puzzle a monkey.' The name stuck.

This long colonnade of monkey puzzles at Bicton near Exeter was once the most admired in Britain. It was planted along the drive to their house by the Rolle family, from seeds imported in 1844 from Chile. The site was windswept and bleak. The trees, bred for the Andes, were happier and grew taller than anywhere else. Within a century the champion was 92 feet high. However, like so many other exotics from the Pacific, the monkey puzzle ages fast in our climate. The Bicton trees grew gaunt and mangy, and some went into a decline. Very sensibly the present owners, Bicton College, replanted with new trees without cutting the old ones – a feat not usually possible.

Since the 1840s a passion for monkey puzzles has swept Britain, and receded. Once they were to be found along the front drive to the most fashionable homes. Now they are considered vulgar – or relegated to the comic section of the garden.

Botanists are surprised by the odd way the scaly whorls develop on the stem. Instead of growing one whorl a year (like pines, spruce, silver fir and so on) they average only about two thirds of a whorl a year. Count 66 'rings' on the trunk of your monkey puzzle and it may be 100 years old.

Another puzzle for monkeys.

The monkey puzzles at Bicton

BACK FROM THE DEAD AT MURTHLY

MURTHLY CASTLE, ASTRIDE THE TAY NEAR DUNKELD,

HAS BRED MANY OF THE MOST ESOTERIC CHAMPION

TREES IN BRITAIN: THE TALLEST SERBIAN SPRUCE, THE

BROADEST SITKA/SERBIAN HYBRID AND SO ON. BUT ITS

MOST STRIKING AND SOMBRE FEATURE IS THE DEAD

WALK LEADING TO THE CHAPEL.

A close walk of 70 common yews, planted some 250 years ago, leads from the castellated house to the chapel. By tradition, the laird of Murthly only passes in this direction once: carried there on his way to the grave. But he is allowed to walk as often as he chooses in the opposite direction.

I photographed the current laird, Robert Steuart-Fothringham, strolling back from the chapel in September 1995. 'Do go back and do that again,' I said thoughtlessly. Had I forgotten he was in the position of Lot's wife, not to speak of Eurydice? One backward step, even a backward glance, could have been the end of him.

Fortunately Robert Steuart-Fothringham was not born yesterday. He walked back to the chapel outside the Dead Walk before returning cheerfully from the grave.

The Dead Walk of yews at Murthly

NEW ZEALAND TO THE RESCUE

IT WAS 1857 AND AN ANCIENT FAMILY, THE CARLYONS OF TREGREHAN IN CORNWALL, WAS IN DISARRAY. THE YOUNGER SON HAD SEDUCED THE COACHMAN'S DAUGHTER. TOLD NEVER TO DARKEN THE DOOR AGAIN, THE YOUNG MAN TOOK REFUGE ON A SHEEP STATION IN NEW ZEALAND, WELL USED TO BLACK SHEEP OF ALL KINDS, AND MADE HIS FORTUNE.

Four generations later the direct line of the Carlyons had failed, and the black sheep's descendant, 23-year-old Tom Hudson, returned to take possession.

He found the famous garden at Tregrehan in tatters. Just as at Heligan, six miles to the south-west, the understorey of *Rhododendron ponticum* had become an overstorey. Worse still, storms from the Atlantic half a mile away had made a battlefield of the arboretum, felling the larger specimens – pines from Monterey, Thuya from the Rockies and so on. Honey fungus was in its element, making a meal of the prostrate trunks and the roots pointing at the sky.

Where to begin? Tom Hudson began by liberating from the jungle the main walk, a double line of Irish yews. The weight of the rhododendrons had crushed these most upright of trees. Tom pruned them up to make a Gothic arcade.

Then he planted hundreds of jewel-like plants that delight in the mild wet winters and the cool wet summers of Cornwall: especially camellias from western China and Japan.

I photographed one shy camellia, a scarlet *japonica*, hesitating on the edge of the yew walk.

The Irish yews at Tregrehan

TOWERS & A TOMB

TIS NOT SMOOTH RICHMOND'S, NOR YET ACTON'S MILL,

NOR WINDSOR CASTLE, NOR YET SHOOTER'S HILL

NOR GROVES, NOR PLAINS, WHICH FURTHER OFF DO STAND

LIKE LANDSCAPES PORTRAY'D BY SOME HAPPY HAND:

BUT A SWIFT VIEW, WHICH MOST DELIGHTED SHOWS,

AND DOTH THEM ALL, AND ALL AT ONCE, DISCLOSE.

Robert Codrington, on the view from the top of the great hollow elm of Hampstead,
reached by a staircase of 42 steps inside the tree (written *c.*1650).

RIGHT Ten feet up the Whittinghame Yew

PLOTTING DARNLEY'S MURDER

YEWS CAN GROW IN ALMOST ANY SOIL AND TAKE ALMOST ANY SHAPE, HOWEVER EXTRAVAGANT. ONE OF THE MOST EERIE GROWS ON STONY GROUND BESIDE THE OLD TOWER HOUSE OF WHITTINGHAME, EAST LOTHIAN – IN THE 16TH CENTURY THE HOME OF LORD MORTON, DARNLEY'S ASSASSIN. THE BOLE IS ONLY 11 FEET IN GIRTH, AND HARDLY MUCH TALLER, BUT THE BRANCHES FORM A VAST DROOPING DOME 60 FEET HIGH AND 400 FEET IN CIRCUMFERENCE.

You enter this arboreal folly as you would enter an igloo, crawling down a tunnel on hands and knees. The tunnel was formed by bending one section of the branches over an iron frame. Once inside you can straighten your back. The main chamber is about 20 feet high and feels rather like a tomb. (I was there during a heatwave in September; in January it would no doubt be exactly like an igloo.) As it was, filtering through the matted branches, the green light created a chilling atmosphere. It took some minutes to set up my tripod and expose a film. I was relieved to crawl back into the sunlight.

It was under the sepulchral shade of this great tree, according to local tradition, that Lord Morton and his fellow conspirators planned the murder of Mary Queen of Scots' second husband, the Earl of Darnley. Then the assassins were foolish enough to get caught. Did they really plan the murder under the tree? In his confession, Lord Morton admitted that it was planned in the 'yard' at Whittinghame – whatever that meant. It was a pity that no one asked him, before they beheaded him, whether he meant the tree.

I would not be surprised to hear that Morton's ghost haunts the yew tree. And I think that the philosopher statesman, Arthur Balfour, Prime Minister from 1902 to 1905, would not have denied the possibility.

The Balfours bought the Whittinghame estate in the 19th century, and it was Arthur Balfour's home for 81 years. Asked by some local antiquarians whether the tree was really the place where Darnley's murder was planned, Balfour replied, 'that it had more historical plausibility about it than many legends'.

The Whittinghame Yew

GIANTS THAT SMELL OF BOOT POLISH

WESTONBIRT – THE PALATIAL ARBORETUM CREATED BY

THE HOLFORD FAMILY IN GLOUCESTERSHIRE AND NOW

RUN BY FOREST ENTERPRISE – BOASTS MANY TALL

TREES, BUT NONE MORE SURPRISING THAN THE

TUBULAR CLUSTER OF INCENSE CEDARS BREAKING THE

SKYLINE BETWEEN THE MAPLE CLEARING AND THE

MAIN DRIVE.

These 16 trees were planted in 1910, just over half a century after the first of these Pacific giants was introduced to Britain. (Both the English name and the Latin name – *Calocedrus decurrens* – are misleading. The genus has nothing to do with the cedar, but is related to the Thuya. The 'incense' refers to the fragrance of the wood, not the leaves, which smell of boot polish. The tallest of the 16 trees is now approaching 100 feet in height.

Yet Sir George Holford planted the trees only 12 feet apart. How the great man must have been teased by his friends. It was a beginner's mistake to plant the giants so close together. But if it was a mistake, it paid off handsomely. The giants grew as stiff and upright as organ pipes. And somehow they stayed separate: 16 separate organ pipes neatly wrapped in bright green, scaly leaves, held vertically to draw the light onto both faces.

I was lucky to catch them myself in a burst of spring sunshine. Holford must have chosen their companions with care – Persian ironwood on one side, Japanese maple on the other – both pale pink in spring and contrasting with the bright green tubes of the incense cedars.

Back at home, in the warm, dry valleys of the western side of the Cascades and other mountains of California and Oregon, the giant has nothing special to recommend it. The tree is an ordinary shape: a typically relaxed Californian, not stiff and upright like Westonbirt's. And its wood soon rots at the heart, so that the lumber trade are not interested (fortunately for the tree).

In Ireland and Scotland, with a cooler and wetter climate, the tree sprawls. My own specimens are Hobbesian: nasty, brutish and short.

Why should the tree be so stiff and elegant at Westonbirt and in other parts of southern England? This has long baffled the experts. For them that must be frustrating, though the mystery did not, I'm sure, worry the Holfords.

The incense cedars at Westonbirt

WEEPERS & CREEPERS

YOUR HEALTH, MASTER WILLOW. CONTRIVE ME A BAT

TO STRIKE A RED BALL; APART FROM THAT

IN THE LAST RESORT I MUST HANG UP MY HARP ON YOU

Louis Macneice, *Tree Party*, 1962.

RIGHT 'Mr Consequa's' Chinese wisteria at Kew

'NO CLIMBER EVER BROUGHT TO THIS COUNTRY', WROTE W. J. BEAN ABOUT THE CHINESE WISTERIA (*WISTERIA*

SINENSIS) IN THE FIRST EDITION OF HIS MAGISTERIAL VOLUMES ON WOODY PLANTS, 'HAS EVER ADDED MORE TO THE

BEAUTY OF GARDENS.' BEAN WAS WRITING ON THE EVE OF THE GREAT WAR, BUT LATER EDITORS SAW NO REASON TO

CHANGE THE SENTENCE.

ANTI-CLOCKWISE AT KEW

Despite the vogue for the Japanese wisteria (*Wisteria floribunda*) which can produce much longer racemes of flowers, the Chinese wisteria has held its own. It is the more boisterous species, growing faster and flowering earlier. In May it deluges a wall or a pergola with mauve or pale lilac flowers. In December the huge bare stems twine together like Medusa's snakes.

But is it a tree? I suppose not – though I shall not resist the temptation to include it. My excuse: sometimes the snake-like trunks can be tree-like in scale – five feet in girth and up to 100 feet in height – although they have to find some long-suffering old tree, or house, to lean on.

Strange to say for a plant that grows so easily in Europe, all our tens of thousands of plants seem to have originated from a single specimen in China. The mother plant grew in the garden of a Chinese tea merchant in Canton, known to Europeans as 'Mr Consequa', whose nephew had brought it from Changchow.

In May 1816 two ships reached England, each with one cutting from Mr Consequa's wisteria. From these two daughter plants more were propagated in turn. The plant in my photographs is the glory of Kew; it dates from about 1820 and is no doubt the oldest-surviving descendant of Mr Consequa's wisteria.

Coming from Canton, on the steamy coast opposite Hong Kong, the wisteria was at first believed to be as tender as a tropical fruit. So this Kew specimen spent the first 40 years of its life inside a circular hothouse. In fact Changchow, the original source of the plant, is in Fukien province in central China, and Fukien is icy cold in winter. By 1860 the penny had dropped at Kew. Hooker could take the wisteria out of the circular hothouse. Anyway the hothouse was being replaced by Decimus Burton's latest masterpiece, the Temperate House.

But by now the wisteria had moulded itself to the cylinder of glass and iron. This is the shape it still maintains, re-sited in 1860 beside the famous ginkgo, and given a new frame the shape of its old hothouse.

In case you are still puzzled by the difference between the Chinese and Japanese wisterias, compare the way the stems twist. The Japanese go clockwise, the Chinese anti-clockwise. I wish I knew what message this is intended to convey.

The Chinese wisteria at Kew

WILLOW PATTERN AT HYDE PARK

By the rivers of Babylon, there we sat down, yea, we wept when we remembered Zion. We hanged our harps upon the willows in the midst thereof.

Psalm 137.

What is the origin of this 100-year-old, elegant, pale green dish mop growing beside the banks of the Serpentine in Hyde Park, London? The story of the hardy modern weeping willow (*Salix x sepulchralis*) is characteristically tangled.

The most famous weeping willow in Europe in the 18th century was Alexander Pope's weeping willow at Twickenham. 'Give me that willow twig,' he is supposed to have told his friend Lady Suffolk, when she showed him a parcel from Spain neatly tied with willow twigs. He planted the twig and it became the celebrated tree in the garden of his villa at Twickenham – ruthlessly cut down in 1801 by a new owner, fed up with having to show Pope's willow to passing tourists.

But this story of the willow from Spain is almost certainly a confusion. So is the actual name, *Salix babylonica*, given the 18th-century tree by the father of modern botany, the great Swedish naturalist, Linnaeus. He was referring to the willows in the psalms, upon which the Children of Israel hanged their harps. We now know that these romantic harp-stands were actually poplars (*Populus euphratica*) mistranslated from the old Hebrew word, *gharab*.

Indeed when botanists sit down, yea, and remember what a mess they've made classifying the weeping willow, it's enough to make them weep.

Let us fight our way back through the jungle of willow stems. *Salix babylonica* originated in China. This is the weeping willow which grows in public parks from Beijing to Shanghai, the tree beside which millions used to do their morning exercises while reciting verses from the Little Red Book of Chairman Mao. It is also the tree we all know from Willow Pattern plates, the tree on the right of the bridge under the two love-birds. Cuttings from this species were apparently brought from China in antiquity, carried in the saddlebags of traders along the Silk Road; but the tree must have reached the Euphrates long after the Children of Israel left it.

Sometime before 1730, a Turkish merchant at Aleppo called Vernon brought cuttings to London and planted one at Twickenham. Cuttings from this tree, not from Lady Suffolk's Spanish parcel, were almost certainly the origin of Pope's willow.

Is this the origin of the modern weeping willow – like this 100-year-old, pale green dish mop on the banks of the Serpentine in Hyde Park?

Yes and no, would be the answer of most modern botanists. The common weeping willow is now a hardy hybrid, *Salix x sepulchralis*, thought to be a cross between the Chinese original, *Salix babylonica*, and a hardy European white willow, *Salix alba*. The new hybrid is hardier and more vigorous, and the young stems, grey in the Chinese original, are often golden in the hybrid (hence the earlier name '*chrysocoma*', meaning golden-haired).

In the chillier parts of Europe, *Salix babylonica* is now rare indeed. Plant a cutting in southern England if you feel daring; it might survive the frost. You might even find a cutting descended from the famous example of *Salix babylonica* growing near Napoleon's grave in St Helena. Before that tree died, cuttings were sent to Napoleon's fans throughout the world.

Best of all, take your *Salix babylonica* cutting direct from China. I expect there's some elegant material from the graves of China's emperors, including Chairman Mao.

The weeping willow at the Serpentine

ONLY A FEW MILES FROM THE CELEBRATED CREMATORIUM, BROOKWOOD NECROPOLIS NEAR WOKING, IS THE BEECH

THAT MIGHT BE AWARDED THE TITLE OF BRITAIN'S DOTTIEST TREE.

MULTIPLYING MOURNERS AT KNAP HILL

It is a huge, weird, weeping beech at Knap Hill nursery, covering half an acre of ground, with a vast dome and numerous separate spires 80 feet high.

No common species has indulged itself with more whimsical forms (mutations or sports to a botanist) than the native European beech, *Fagus sylvatica*. There are cheerful beeches with golden leaves ('Zlatia'), romantic beeches with fern-like leaves ('Asplenifolia'), gloomy beeches with purple leaves ('Purpurea') and incongruous combinations of crinkly, purple, fern-like leaves ('Rohanii').

The Knap Hill weeping beech, *Fagus sylvatica* 'Pendula', is the most extravagant. In the 1820s it was apparently imported from France, one of the first to reach Britain, and planted in what was already Waterer's well-known nursery. Not content with its own mournful form it then proceeded to multiply mourners at an alarming rate. To do that by seed would have been impossible.

Mutations that breed sexually normally revert to type. So the mutation rebelled. Each branch of the Knap Hill beech 'layered', that is, formed a new weeping beech where it touched the ground. The oldest branches have formed new weeping beeches 80 feet high; others swoop and droop and hug in crazy confusion.

You can see the multiplication process in my photograph. In the foreground is the original trunk, divided in two at the base; at the back the cascade of branches forming new trees.

Originally there were five of these weeping beeches imported to Knap Hill. Imagine the crisis if all five had rebelled. But four behaved sensibly. Only this one turned into a weeping wood.

The Knap Hill weeping beech

ROOTERY AT WAKEHURST

> ...nor tree
> Grows here, but what is fed with Magick Juice
> All full of humane Souls; that cleave their barks
> To dance at Midnight by the Moon's pale beams.

Nathaniel Lee, *Oedipus*

At Wakehurst, Kew's romantic outpost in Sussex, there is a pleasantly sinister path through the woods known as the 'Rock Walk'. Nothing much is known about its origin. It appears to have been made in the early 19th century by cutting through the miniature cliffs of sandstone which geologists call 'Ardingly Beds'. You are supposed to have a Gothick frisson, to sniff the air of dungeon and graveyard, when you follow this path. Thick, black yews, natural to these woods, contrast with the greeny-blue, theatrical shapes of the sandstone (*see right*). You expect a grotto, and perhaps a skeleton or two. But there is nothing to speak of – not even a stuffed hermit.

Then you see, as your eyes adjust to the gloom, that there *is* something menacing about the place. The yews have walked – or rather scuttled or slithered – over these greeny-blue cliffs to reach new soil. It is a Rootery, not a Rockery – and a snake-pit.

Of course they have been driven to it by erosion. Two hundred Sussex winters have washed the rocks as bare of soil as stage scenery. But I don't advise a trip by moonlight if you intend to pay your respects to these wandering, naked roots.

The yews on the rocks
at Wakehurst

PART FIVE

SURVIVORS

RELICS & RUINS

YOU ARE NO RUIN, SIR – NO LIGHTNING-STRUCK TREE: YOU ARE

GREEN AND VIGOROUS. PLANTS WILL GROW ABOUT YOUR ROOTS,

WHETHER YOU ASK THEM OR NOT.

Jane Eyre to Mr Rochester after he had lost his sight in the fire.
From *Jane Eyre* by Charlotte Brontë.

PREVIOUS PAGE 'Dodders' in Windsor Great Park

RIGHT First choice for Herne's Oak

HUNTING HERNE'S OAKS AT WINDSOR

Mrs Page:

> There is an old tale goes, that Herne the hunter,
> Sometime a keeper here in Windsor Forest,
> Doth all the winter time, at still midnight,
> Walk round about an oak, with great ragged horns,
> And there he blasts a tree.

Shakespeare, *The Merry Wives of Windsor,* Act IV, Scene IV.

Herne the hunter, the keeper of Windsor Forest, hanged himself from an oak tree, then haunted the spot. That is the tale that was already old in Shakespeare's time. But can the tree once known as Herne's Oak be identified today?

It would certainly be odd if a tree already 'blasted' in the 16th century could be found, dead or alive, four centuries later. But almost anything seems possible with these 'dodders' – the traditional name for the ancient pollard oaks of Windsor Great Park.

There are more than 100 of these ancient trees along the main road, the A332, that bisects the park. In 1864, William Menzies, the Surveyor of Windsor Park, produced a vast folio

Second candidate for Herne's Oak

volume which lists the trees then surviving; from this it is clear that the 'dodders' predate the planting of oaks for timber that began, at Lord Burleigh's suggestion, in 1580.

In short, the 'dodders' are self-sown oaks from the Middle Ages. Yet few of the tourists, who flock to Windsor to see the sights, even bother to turn their heads, as they speed past – indeed it might be dangerous if they did.

But which dodder is Herne's dodder?

In 1838, John Claudius Loudon, in his monumental *Arboretum Britannicum*, listed two possible Herne's Oaks in Windsor park. Both were already dead and neither can be found today.

My own feeling is that, if Herne's Oak doesn't exist it needs to be invented. So here are three possible candidates.

They were photographed in February and March 1996 soon after dawn. The one whose face is coated with hoar-frost has the most Herne-like expression. He has my vote.

Hunting Herne's Oaks at dawn can be chilly work, and one is on swampy ground, historically speaking. One reaches firmer ground with William the Conqueror's Oak, long regarded as even older than Herne's Oak – indeed the oldest oak in the forest.

It stands opposite the pink lodge at Cranborne Gate, on the edge of a young oak wood, including perhaps some of its descendants. It has probably been in a state of collapse for at least two centuries, yet still carries several tons of young branches above its hollow trunk, 27 feet in circumference.

'We lunched in it', wrote Professor Burnet, 'on September 2 1829: it would accommodate at least 20 persons with standing room, and ten or 12 might sit comfortably down to dinner. I think at Willis's and in Guildhall I have danced a quadrille in a smaller space.'

The Conqueror's Oak is now jealously guarded by the Crown Estate Commissioners, who control the park. When I went to see it, I was stopped by a man with a walkie-talkie who asked me what I was doing. He seemed relieved to hear I was taking photographs, not planning to sit down to dinner with ten or 12 persons inside – or dance a quadrille.

ABOVE LEFT William the Conqueror's Oak

RIGHT Third candidate for Herne's Oak

EVELYN'S 'GREAT CHESTNUT'

BY FAR THE MOST FULLY DOCUMENTED ANCIENT TREE

IN BRITAIN IS THE HUGE CONFUSED SWEET CHESTNUT

BESIDE THE PARISH CHURCH OF TORTWORTH,

GLOUCESTERSHIRE. UNFORTUNATELY THE DOCUMEN-

TATION IS AS CONFUSED AS THE TREE.

It is clear that the species, *Castanea sativa*, was imported – perhaps it was brought by the Romans for the sake of the nuts. It is native to the mountains of southern Europe. On Mount Etna there is an old monster, the Tree of a Hundred Horses, known to tourists since the Renaissance. But how old is the monster at Tortworth? John Evelyn, writing in 1664, claimed the 'great chestnut' had been a boundary tree in the 12th century.

We first glimpse Tortworth in Kip's birds-eye view, reproduced in Sir Robert Atkyns' *Ancient and Present state of Gloucestershire* (1712). The tree is growing beside a garden wall. Atkyns writes: 'there is a remarkable chestnut tree growing in the garden, belonging to the manor house, which by tradition is said to have been growing there in the reign of King John (13th century); it is nineteen yards in compass, and seems to be several trees

incorporated together; and young ones are still growing up which may in time be joined to the old body.'

More details of its apparent age were given half a century later by Peter Collinson, Britain's leading amateur dendrologist, writing in the *Gentleman's Magazine* for 1762 and 1766. The great chestnut at 'Tortsworth (sic) alias Tamworth' was 'in all probability ...the oldest, if not the largest tree in England, being 52 feet round'. Collinson dated it, on somewhat shaky ground, to the 9th century: 'I may with reason fix its rising from the nut in the reign of King Egbert, anno 800.'

The 19th century saw the tree rise to its apotheosis. It was engraved by Jacob Strutt (*see left*), lithographed by Georgina Moreton, serenaded by an anonymous poet (whose doggerel is still visible, engraved on a plaque by the tree). However it was already such a baffling combination of old wood and new wood, as predicted by Atkyns a century before, that no two people could agree on its size. Where did the original trunk end and the new trunks begin? In 1791 its girth was declared to be 44 feet 4 inches. In 1825

Strutt measured the tree at 52 feet or did he just borrow Collinson's measurements from the previous century? Strutt repeated the claim that it was probably the oldest tree standing in England.

Today the great chestnut is a riot. The old walls have vanished. Someone has fenced off the tree to protect it from cattle. This has allowed new trunks and new branches to burst out in all directions. The old trunk is now 36 feet in girth according to my tape measure: more like a waterfall than a tree; huge, half-rotten, yet bursting with new life – including some surplus nuts that I have planted in my garden.

The mystery of its age remains. How old would a tree be now that was a 'great chestnut' in John Evelyn's day? Not the oldest tree in Britain. Collinson and Strutt were wrong there: yews are the ultimate winners in the survival stakes. Loudon thought the Romans must have planted it. That must be wrong, too. But the main trunk could be 1,100 years old, that is, old in the time of King Stephen – even if we need not follow Collinson all the way back to King Egbert's nut.

THE PRISONERS OF CROM

Naturam expelles furca, tamen usque recurret.
(You can drive out nature with a pitchfork, but she always returns.)

Horace.

The 'great yew of Crom' – beside the ruins of the old castle of Crom on the shores of Lough Erne, County Fermanagh – features in several books by experts, including Elwes and Henry's, who should have known better.

There are actually two great yews of Crom a few paces apart, a male yew and a female yew, twins in fact, yet far from identical, each a giant freak of a kind, though surprisingly little known to the public.

I showed the photograph of the male twin to a camper whose brightly coloured tent had been pitched just beyond the dark green circle of branches. 'What do you think of it?' I asked. 'Amazing', she replied. 'Where is it? Far from here? I'd like to see that.' 'Twenty feet away.' It took her some time to grasp that this wonder of the world

was not in another part of Ireland, but a few paces from where we stood.

From outside, it is true, you have no idea that there are two trees. All you see is a matted dome of branches in the abandoned garden of the old castle beside Lough Erne. Inside, there is a scene of Baroque confusion, partially resolved by some recent crude pruning commissioned by the National Trust, who now own this part of the estate.

The twins were apparently planted in the 17th century, by an ancestor of the present Lord Erne, to make a Baroque garden for his castle. Both were cut back in the prevailing style of formal gardening. The twin brother was pruned in the form of a hedge (*see above*). The twin sister (the one with scarlet berries – *see left*) was pinioned on a

wooden frame and strapped down to 34 brick pillars. Under its black shade – more like a dungeon than a summer-house, one would have thought – Lord Erne would entertain his friends.

About 1833, the Lord Erne of the day relented; at least the 34 brick pillars were replaced with 16 oak posts. Then he died, and the next Lord Erne abandoned the summer-house. He built himself a new castle half a mile away down the shore of the lake, and the twin yews were left to return to nature.

Hence the liberated freaks we have today. Nature has broken out of the formal hedge and the summer-house (with one post still visible) in glorious abandon.

I hope the National Trust have finished their pruning. It would be sad to see the brother and sister returned to their prison.

A REFUGE BY THE RUNWAY

LIKE MOST ANCIENT YEWS LEFT IN BRITAIN, THE HARLINGTON YEW HAS FOUND REFUGE IN A CHURCHYARD (*SEE LEFT*). BUT IT IS AN ODD REFUGE: A SMALL OASIS BETWEEN THE VILLAGE CHURCH, AN OLD CEDAR, THE SOUTHERN LANES OF THE M4 MOTORWAY AND (ONLY A MILE AWAY) THE EAST END OF THE RUNWAYS AT HEATHROW AIRPORT.

In the 18th century the tree was reckoned to be 80 feet high, and one of the tallest, if not *the* tallest, yews in Europe. It was used as a kind of church tower.

> Welcome whether foul or Fair
> To climb up her all Comers are;
> And as from top of Monument
> To view the Town and all that's in't.

The author of this ditty of 1729, illustrated here, was said to be John Saxy, the man employed to prune the tree.

> Masters if you approve these Lays
> And shaver Saxy deign to praise
> Crown him with Yew instead of Bays.
> Be kind to John your tree who trims
> With easy Rhimes, but aching limbs.

John Saxy must have earned his keep. He had to prune the tree as a piece of topiary 80 feet high, to clip its double row of hoops, pyramid, globe and weathercock on top. He does not tell us its age; presumably he had no idea. It was already 'immortal', for it was completely hollow.

> Tis strange! but she immortal grows
> With Age, that spoils all other Beaux.
> Within, tis true, She's not so sound,
> But hollow from the top to ground.

Of course fancy dress for trees was passing out of fashion. When a new flint-and-stone church tower was built at the beginning of the 19th century, the tree was allowed to revert to ordinary dress.

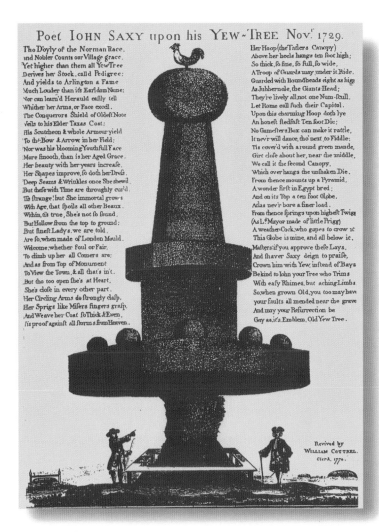

The Harlington Yew in 1729

But old age has not been kind to it. The tree is now only half the height it was two centuries ago, and half its lower trunk has mouldered away. But if you make a trip to Harlington on a summer evening, braving the roar of cars and aeroplanes, you can still see the ghost of Saxy's topiary of 1729: the line of the lower hoop, ten feet from the ground, clearly visible on the right of the photograph.

A FAMILY PET AT BOWTHORPE

Time made thee what thou wast, King of the woods,
And time hath made thee what thou art, a cave
For owls to roost in...

William Cowper, *The Yardley Oak,* 1791

In May 1996 I paid my respects to Bowthorpe in Lincolnshire in what was to be the final journey made for this book.

By comparison with its co-champion oak, 'Majesty' at Fredville (see page 19), the Bowthorpe Oak (*right and below*) looks like Methuselah. It is a cave with branches growing from the roof. Is it 1,000 years old, as one expert, Alan Mitchell, suggested? All that we know is that in 1768 it had 'been in the same state of decay since the memory of the older inhabitants and their ancestors'. The hollow trunk was then smoothed out to make a room in which the squire of Bowthorpe Park could sit down to dinner with 20 friends.

The squires of Bowthorpe Park have long vanished. The current owner, an industrious farmer called Alec Blanchard, took me proudly to the tree, across the field from his terrace and swimming pool. I caught my breath. It seemed to fill the field. In the past he has used the tree as a stable. 'That's where a New Forest pony got its head stuck. We had to rope it to get it out.'

When I came back with my camera, his six grandchildren – Josh, Rebecca, Emma, Nick, George and

Harriette – joined the party. They showed off the tree as though it was a family pet. They stroked it, petted it, climbed it – and out flew a roosting bird, a Little Owl, they said. Then we went inside. The trunk had a doorway cut in it, which has partly closed itself in the last 200 years. Was there really room for 20 to dine inside? The children assured me there was; and we measured the dining room, nine by six at present.

We looked at the graffiti cut into the smooth inner walls, for which the worms have shown little respect. Eric told me he had found some inscriptions dating from the 18th century. The earliest I could find dated from 1816. There were also more modern messages.

I thought of Cowper's poem on the ruined oak at Yardley, 'a cave for owls'. The Bowthorpe Oak is a cave for Clive to tell Carol he loves her to distraction.

PRAYING FOR GILBERT WHITE'S YEW

EVER SINCE THE REVEREND GILBERT WHITE PUBLISHED

HIS *NATURAL HISTORY AND ANTIQUITIES OF SELBORNE* IN

1789, THE ANCIENT YEW IN THE CHURCHYARD AT

SELBORNE, HAMPSHIRE HAS BEEN ONE OF THE BEST-

KNOWN YEWS IN ENGLAND. WE ARE TOLD BY GILBERT

WHITE THAT IT WAS ALREADY 23 FEET IN CIRCUM-

FERENCE AT THREE FEET FROM THE GROUND: SHORT

AND SQUAT, WITH A HABIT OF THROWING OUT POLLEN

IN APRIL (AS MALE YEWS WILL) UNEXPECTEDLY OVER HIS

PARISHIONERS.

Nearly 200 years later Alan Mitchell, Britain's leading tree enthusiast, put his tape round it and found it had grown so slowly – only three feet in 200 years – that he reckoned it was 1,400 years old.

If Mitchell was right, the great yew of Selborne, like many ancient yews in churchyards with similar or even larger dimensions, predated its local church by hundreds of years and may have been a holy tree from the time of the Druids. A few years after Mitchell's visit, archaeological excavations confirmed that the tree did predate the earliest burials in that part of the churchyard.

For, sad to say, the tree which had survived so many trials was finally flattened by the great wind of January 1990. At first the vicar hoped that he could restore the stricken tree to life. He must have been reading his copy of White's *Selborne*, for White tells the story there of how, after the great storm of 1703, the parishioners tried to re-erect a huge, fallen oak tree, which had been 'the delight of old and young...where the former sat in grave debate while the latter frolicked and danced'.

In 1990 the vicar and his parishioners gently cut off the head of the great yew. Then, with a borrowed crane, the headless trunk was hauled back into position. A notice, penned by the vicar, exhorted the faithful to pray for the tree. Flickers of life were indeed apparent: the fresh green of young foliage sprouting from its battered midriff. But the flickers faded – exactly as they had faded when Gilbert White's predecessors had tried to restore their giant oak to life 300 years earlier.

When I took my photograph the vicar's prayers did not seem to have been answered, but the tree has been left (very sensibly) to serve as a beetle-infested monument to Gilbert White, who loved beetles as much as he loved trees.

The yew at Selborne

DEATH
AT
CHATSWORTH

Three centuries he grows, and three he stays,
Supreme in state, and in three more decays.

Dryden.

Three hundred years growing
Three hundred years living
Three hundred years dying.

The life of an oak, according to an old saying.

It is 1845: for the poor the depths of the Hungry Forties, for the rich the golden age of treemanship. William George Spencer Cavendish, 6th Duke of Devonshire, the Bachelor Duke, and blessed with more cash than many European monarchs, is conducting tourists round the new pinetum at Chatsworth, most splendid of his seven family homes.

He describes this tour in the *Handbook for Chatsworth* that he wrote that year. He is in high spirits, and can be pardoned a touch of self-satisfaction. Together he and Joseph Paxton have made the garden at Chatsworth the most famous in Britain.

The hemlock spruces are very fine, and there is a tall larch, which the old house-keeper remembered to have been brought in a pot from Welbeck as a curiosity. Near the water there is a good specimen of *Araucaria imbricata* [monkey-puzzle], the oldest I have got. That is the Douglas pine [Douglas fir], the pride of California: in 1829 it came down

in Mr Paxton's hat, and in 1845 it is 35 feet high... This ground is ... much admired but no two of a party take the same view of it; one extols the scenery, another is in raptures at the old oaks...

How characteristic of the Duke to remember the old oaks – the oldest retainers on his estate. Their age makes even the Cavendish family look parvenus; the oaks must have already seen centuries of service when the Cavendishes reached Chatsworth in the 16th century.

Today these old retainers have been pensioned off in the old deer park, secure from intruders behind a locked gate. Their sanctuary is just behind the Victorian pinetum. I was taken there by their keeper, who is also responsible for the deer. The trees are even more extraordinary – more poetic, more Gothic – than the Queen's dodders in Windsor Great Park.

Out of their caves in the bracken, where the hinds put their fawns for safety, rise 100 ancient oaks, tier on tier up the steep hillside. Most appear medieval: that is, they have reached the final 300 years of their life – the '300 years dying'. Some are already dead, and stand corpse-like, with hands outstretched. I have chosen two of them for my photograph.

'You should see them at the full moon', says the deer park keeper, 'the trees look at you in an odd way.' I thought they looked at us quite oddly enough in full sunlight.

Oaks at Chatsworth

THE
NEWCOMER

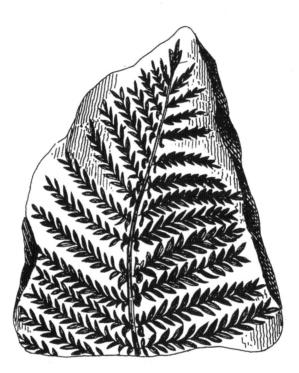

'THERE MUST BE A GOD IN THE TREE,' A SIXTY-YEAR-OLD VILLAGER

TOLD US THROUGH AN INTERPRETER, 'IT'S THE BIGGEST,

STRONGEST, STRAIGHTEST TREE FOR MANY DAYS TRAVEL, BIGGER

THAN ANY OTHER WE HAVE SEEN.'

Milton Silverman, *The Search for Dawn Redwoods* (1990).

RIGHT Metasequoia at the Botanic Garden, Cambridge

Metasequoia at Emmanuel
College, Cambridge

THE OLD TREE FROM MO-TAO-CHI

TO DISCOVER A 'LIVING FOSSIL' – A TREE PREVIOUSLY

ONLY KNOWN FROM FOSSILIZED SPECIMENS OF TREES

THAT HAD DIED MILLIONS OF YEARS BEFORE – WOULD

HAVE BEEN EXCITING ANYWAY. BUT THE DISCOVERY OF

THE *METASEQUOIA GLYPTOSTROBOIDES* (ALIAS 'DAWN

REDWOOD') IN CHINA IN 1941 WAS OUTSTANDING FOR

ANOTHER REASON. THIS TURNED OUT TO BE THE ONLY

IMPORTANT HARDY GENUS OF TREE DISCOVERED IN

THE ENTIRE 20TH CENTURY.

It is true that in 1994 a sensational new genus, the Wollemi Pine, was discovered in the Blue Mountains, an hour's drive from Sydney, Australia. This, too, is a living fossil. But it is unlikely that it will prove hardy in our climate – that is, could flourish out of doors in Britain or Ireland.

The three metasequoias I have photographed for this book are growing vigorously in Cambridge, and are already over 60 feet high, although only planted in 1948, grown from the first consignment of seed sent from China.

The story of the discovery of the tree reads like a botanical thriller. In 1941, in wartime Japan, a palaeobotanist called Shigeru Miki was peering into his microscope one day when he noticed something odd about fossil specimens from America labelled '*sequoia*' (coastal redwood) and '*taxodium*' (swamp cypress). The paired leaves were alternate not opposite, as in the swamp cypress. In due course he published an article claiming that he had found a new fossil genus, and christened it '*metasequoia*' (meaning 'like the sequoia').

Three thousand miles away, that same year, the Red Army partisans led by Mao were licking their wounds in western China, after retreating from the Japanese invaders. One day a young man called T. Kan was sent to check available supplies of firewood at Mo-tao-chi, a small village close to the Yangtse in eastern Sichuan. He was a forester by training and was puzzled by the sight of an old conifer beside the village temple. The villagers called it a 'water fir', but this meant nothing to him. As the tree was deciduous, he waited till spring, then asked the local schoolmaster to collect leaf specimens and send them to him. The specimens were sent – and lost. The years rolled on. It was not until 1946 that specimens reached Professor Hu, head of a botanical institute in Beijing, who had read

Miki's article written in 1941. Professor Hu reached a conclusion he found astounding. Here was Miki's metasequoia alive and well in Mo-tao-chi three million years after it had died out in the rest of the world. He christened it *glyptostroboides,* meaning 'like a *glyptostrobus,* the Chinese swamp cypress'.

However in 1946 the Chinese economy was in such a fragile state that no one in Beijing could afford to pay a collector to bring back seeds from the newly discovered tree.

In 1947 American botanists came to the rescue. For the paltry sum of $250, the Arnold Arboretum at Harvard sponsored a Chinese expedition to Mo-tao-chi. By January 1948 seed packets were being sent to botanical gardens all over the world. And rescue came just in time. The next year Mao's Red Army took over China, and the bamboo curtain came down with a crash, cutting off Chinese botanists from the West for the next 29 years.

Meanwhile, freedom tasted wonderful to the metasequoia. The tree whose world had shrunk to a single valley in eastern Sichuan (and a few neighbouring valleys, it later emerged) was born again in every temperate region of the world. Its appetite for life was extraordinary. Rocky soils, chalky soils, acid bogs: nothing seemed to daunt it. From the old tree at Mo-tao-chi hundreds of thousands of young trees were propagated and planted in Europe and North America. These were the regions where it grew three million years before.

The finest trio I know in Britain are these three at Cambridge, the first photographed in spring at Emmanuel College, the other two in autumn at the Botanic Garden.

I cannot recommend the tree too highly if you want a specimen for your lawn. Its leaves turn pink in autumn. It looks like an American swamp cypress, but grows twice as fast, and is more tolerant of lime.

One word of warning. No one can say how high your metasequoia will grow. Already the tree has reached 91 feet at Leonardslee in Sussex. I am sure it is glad to be back in Europe and America. And it is impatient. It has a lot of lost time – three million years – to make up.

The second metasequoia at the Botanic Garden, Cambridge

GAZETTEER

BIBLIOGRAPHY

Note: All books printed in London unless otherwise stated.

The Gardener's Chronicle
The Gardener's Magazine
The Garden 1-120
International Dendrology Society Yearbook 1966-95,
    Kew 1991-6
Bean, W.J. and eds., *Trees and Shrubs Hardy in the British Isles,* 4 vols and
    supp., (8th edn., 1976).
Bourdu, Robert, *Arbres Souverains* (Paris, 1988).
Bretschneider, Emil, *History of European Botanical Discoveries in China*
    (Reprint, Leipzig 1962).
Chetan, A. and Brueton, D, *The Sacred Yew* (1994).
Cox, E.H.M., *Plant Hunting in China* (1945).
Desmond, R., *Dictionary of British and Irish Botanists and Horticulturalists*
    (1977).
Elliot, Brent, *Victorian Gardens* (1986).
Elwes, H. and Henry, A., *The Trees of Great Britain and Ireland* (Edinburgh
    1906-13).
Evelyn, John, *Sylva or a Discourse on Forest Trees* (1st edn., 1664, Dr A.
    Hunter's edn. 1776).
Fisher, J., *The Origins of Garden Plants* (1982).
Fowles, John, *The Tree* (1979).
Griffiths, Mark, *Index of Garden Plants. The New R.H.S. Dictionary*
    (Portland, Oregon 1994).
Hayes, Samuel, *A Practical Treatise on Planting* (Dublin 1794).
Hillier Ltd, *Hillier's Manual of Shrubs and Trees* (5th edn., 1989).
Howard, Alexander, *Trees in Britain* (1946).
Hunt, John Dixon, *The Figure in the Landscape* (Baltimore 1989).
Hussey, Christopher, *English Gardens and Landscapes (1700-1750)* (1967).
Jackson, A.B., *Catalogue of the Trees and Shrubs of Westonbirt* (Oxford 1927).
Johnson, Hugh, *The International Book of Trees* (1973).
Lamb, K. and Bowe, P., *A History of Gardening in Ireland* (Dublin 1995).

Lowe, J., *The Yew Trees of Great Britain and Ireland* (1897).
Loudon, John Claudius, *Arboretum et Fruticetum Britannicum,* 8 vols, (2nd
    edn, 1844).
Malins, E. and Knight of Glin, *Lost Demesnes* (1976).
Menninger, E.A., *Fantastic Trees* (Reprint, Portland, Oregon 1995).
Menzies, William, *Windsor Forest as Described in Ancient and Modern Poets*
    (1875).
Menzies, William, *A History of Windsor Great Park* (1864).
Miller, Philip, *Gardener's Dictionary* (8th edn., 1768).
Milner, Edward, *The Tree Book* (1992).
Mitchell, Alan, *The Trees of Britain and Northern Europe* (Reprint,
    Collins/Domino 1989).
Mitchell, Alan, *The Complete Guide to the Trees of Britain and Northern
    Europe* (1985).
Mitchell, Alan, *A Field Guide to the Trees of Britain and Northern Europe*
    (Reprint, 1979).
Mitchell, Alan F. etc, *Champion Trees in the British Isles* (Forestry
    Commission, 4th edn., 1994).
Nelson, E.C. and Walsh, W., *The Trees of Ireland* (Dublin 1993).
Pim, Sheila, *The Wood and the Trees. A Biography of Augustine Henry* (2nd
    edn., Kilkenny 1984).
Rackham, Oliver, *The History of the Countryside* (1986).
Ravenscroft, Edward J., *The Pinetum Britannicum* (Edinburgh and London
    1863-84).
Rushton, Keith, *Conifers* (1987).
Selby, P.J., *A History of British Forest Trees* (1842).
Spongberg, Stephen A., *A Re-Union of Trees* (1990).
Strutt, Jacob, *Sylva Britannica or Portraits of Forest Trees* (Folio edn., 1826).
Thomas, Keith, *Man and the Natural World,* (1983).
Wilks, J.H., *Trees of the British Isles in History and Legend* (1972).
Wilson, E.H., *A Naturalist in Western China,* 2 vols, (1913).
Wood, P. (ed.), *The Tree: A Celebration of Our Living Skyline* (1990).
Young, Andrew, *A Retrospect of Flowers* (1950).

ILLUSTRATIONS

Background illustrations by J. Miller, 1776, from Hunter's edition of *Sylva*
by J. Evelyn.

INDEX

First published in 1996 by
George Weidenfeld & Nicolson Ltd

This paperback edition first published in 1997 by
Phoenix Illustrated
Orion Publishing Group, Orion House
5, Upper St. Martin's Lane
London WC2H 9EA

British Library Cataloguing-in-Publication Data
A catalogue record for this book is available from
the British Library

ISBN 0-75380-237-6

Printed and bound in Italy